Women of the Shadows

Women of the Shadows

by Ann Cornelisen

Photographs by the Author

VINTAGE BOOKS
A Division of Random House
New York

FIRST VINTAGE BOOKS EDITION
March 1977
Copyright © 1976 by Ann Cornelisen

All rights reserved under International and Pan-American Copyright Conventions. Published in the United States by Random House, Inc., New York, and simultaneously in Canada by Random House of Canada Limited, Toronto. Originally published by Atlantic-Little, Brown Brooks, Little, Brown and Company in association with The Atlantic Monthly Press, in 1976.

Library of Congress Cataloging in Publication Data
Cornelisen, Ann, 1926-
Women of the shadows.

1. Women—Italy, Southern.
2. Italy, Southern—Social conditions.
I. Title.
[HQ1644.S6C6   1977]   301.41′2′09457
76-49461
ISBN 0-394-72345-7

Author's Note

Peppina, Ninetta, Teresa and Maria all exist. They have names and faces and families. They do what they must; they struggle today, as in the past. Pinuccia and Cettina exist too and have names, faces and families. They are younger. Their lives are less set; they still have their way to find. All have done things of which they are not proud, and if they know in their hearts, as one woman said, that nothing is private, they would also agree with her conclusion: That doesn't mean you get used to it. Since to me their lives, not their names, are important, and I wish to respect their privacy, I have invented names for them that have no relation to their own, and I hope to no one else's.

The photographs were taken in Southern Italy, primarily in Lucania, over a period of years. Some are of people I know, others, of people whom I have seen only once — through a camera lens — and to whom I may never have spoken. In no case are they of people mentioned in the text or of the places those people live.

The choice of one word rather than any other is entirely subjective. Words form sentences and ultimately paragraphs which, in spite of the writer's best efforts, will always reflect his perceptions, even his interpretations and prejudices. Nor is the camera more obliging: they say it does not lie, but its truth is what the photographer chose to see and how he chose to see it. I make no claim to objectivity, desirable as it may be. When one human being describes another human being objectivity is, by its very definition, impossible. I have known these women for years. I respect them, like them, dislike them, am amused, irritated and enraged by them. We have laughed together and sometimes cried. And so, though I believe in the objective truth of what I have written, I must also accept that it is subjective.

Contents

Women of the Shadows

Introduction

Perhaps there will always be one last word I want to say about Southern Italy. After twenty years I accept my allegiance to it, my voluntary bondage as a chronic, even pernicious affinity which familiarity and disappointment have not cured and which neither absence nor bitterness can weaken. Norman Douglas, who wrote so delightfully (and so accurately) about the South, is my consolation. He suffered from the same fascination and must have accepted it as an inconvenient malaise which, though never fatal, imposes its own quarantine. Italians dismiss the opinions and attachments of foreigners: how could we understand this primitive subcontinent of theirs which remains impenetrable to them? No one else cares. Like most obsessions it is a lonely one. I cannot explain it logically, but only sense that what holds me is the odd, almost fatal symmetry of life in the isolated mountains—for that is the South which has always moved me. They suit each other, this bleak land and dour people who see no joy in this life, but only an eternal struggle which they cannot quite win.

The South's is *not* the gentle, terraced landscape of Renaissance painting. It is a bare, sepia world, a cruel world

1

of jagged, parched hills, dry river beds and distant villages where clumps of low houses cling together on the edges of cutbanks. These villages have a certain pattern about them. At one end a long gray barracks, the elementary school, seems to teeter precariously on columns of spongy soil, all that is left between the flumes of erosion. One more winter of rain and the wall must sag, then crumble slowly down toward the valley. At the other end of town a four story "skyscraper," straight and arrogant in its finery of mosaic tiles and plastic panels, serves as an exclamation point: this is the end. In between the bureaucrats reign — government clerks, teachers, priests, police — and those aspiring to such nobility. They live as near the Piazza as they can afford in buildings which, locally, are called palaces, but are of uniform discomfort and disrepair. Peasants live in the lower world, a maze of narrow cobbled streets and dank two-room houses. They are not really part of life here; they merely pause for the dark hours of the night. In the cemetery, away from the town and below it, are the only trees, a few cypress, black scars on the clay. Trees are despised in the South, but cypress may guard the dead.

Twenty years ago (when I first came there) the living seemed in constant motion. The men and their women plied the paths between the villages and the minuscule fields, hauling grain or grapes or fodder, olives and wood, like chains of ants patiently stumbling after each other, determined to transport thousands of crumbs to an invisible lair behind a stone. Now, in the '70's, there are fewer people and fewer donkeys to click the rhythm of their perpetual march. Some of the men no longer go out to the fields but are content to roost on the low stone walls in front of the church or opposite the market. Bad weather drives them into the back rooms of cafés and wine shops, where they pull their caps a little lower to avoid the glare from a neon tube and slouch in chairs, listening half asleep to the monotonous grunts and boasts of other men playing cards. Those who still go to the fields are older. They are the ones who stayed at home. To them the factories of

Milan and Germany were more frightening than the stingy land of Lucania. The women have had no such choice, nor even the luxury of fear. As they have for centuries, young and old alike, they leave for the fields in the false light of dawn and return at dusk, plodding slowly, heavily, stopping occasionally to shift their loads.

They are provident by nature, these women of the South, unable to let even ten square meters of land lie fallow. The land is their insurance against the caprices of an industrialized world they do not understand or trust. Their pessimism has been justified, it seems, for, as the factories of the North adjust to economic recession, their men are coming back and trying once more to buy land, not out of love, but out of fear, and so perhaps the cycle begins again.

In such places land holds a mysterious sway over life. It is food — or money: in the past it was the symbol of power. Even the poorest clay is everything or nothing, depending on man's ability to exploit it. Small wonder peasants watch it with cold, suspicious eyes and talk of disaster in the spring when the wheat shoots are tender and green and the barren slopes that are their only pastures are tufted with wiry bunchgrass. Spring can masquerade in the gay yellow of broom and the lacy blue blossoms of rosemary and wild flowers, scattered like confetti along the verges of the road, but these are only trappings to fool the innocent. The peasants' distrust is contagious. Now, after so many seasons, I realize that for me the southern landscape is most beautiful when it is scorched, when the smoke from burning stubble drifts heavily upward into a violet-red twilight sky which will slowly, almost imperceptibly darken to purple. Then when it promises nothing, we must make our peace with the land.

Life in a Southern Italian village is exclusive of all other life. Distances are great, transportation expensive and difficult. No one seems to have friends in other villages, and cities are places you go to when you need a permit or special medical examinations. In time some subliminal influence relates austerity to good and frivolity to evil. (I remember driving once to the nearest city just to take a bath and see a film and on my return feeling so guilty that I invented "official" errands to explain my absence to neighbors who would never have thought of questioning me.) That I was there by choice and Southern Italians are not, that I could leave at any time, they could not, is incidental. As long as I stayed I was committed to a very particular, circumscribed life. There was no other choice, or so it seemed. I shared what there was, including food of poor quality at high prices, capricious utilities, a wretched climate and the disdain of every outsider. Money could not buy comfort, much less delicacies or amusements.

The town hall, post office and school had wood-burning stoves, water two hours a day, and enough electricity to make a bulb glow dimly in the darkest hours of the night, when there was no one to use it. Modern public housing supplied a stove flue for each apartment, but no heat, and when the pressure was low, no water even for the few precious hours we could expect. The old stone one- or two-room houses each had a chimney, rather like a snorkel, that poked its way to the surface at the front door or bedroom window of the house just above. Women waited in long lines at fountains, if their need for water happened to coincide with the erratic schedule of the aqueduct, and they dumped their slops down street drains from hip-high ceramic jars, called "Zio Pepes," which served them as toilets, but which had a brief and for me disconcerting vogue in the cities as umbrella stands.

My life could not be very different. I rented an apartment in one of the barracks-like buildings that the first post-war governments had thought appropriate housing for peasants. There were no stalls, no storerooms. Chickens, even piglets, roamed the stairways, and bicycles, push-carts and scooters which had, perforce, replaced the donkeys, clogged the entrances. One of the few benefits of these modern units was a

Sitz bath where I could store water. I bailed it into the toilet, into the basin for the patchy sponge baths that I could manage, and I boiled it for my pasta. I too had a wood-burning stove that I lighted on those evenings when the wind was not gusting down the flue. If in the winter at lunchtime I wanted to read for a few minutes, I went to my car (in that I was unique) and ran the motor until the heater worked. My only other choice would have been to sit at the local baker's, but no one would have allowed me to read: that is the place to meet your friends for a good gossip. Since on Sundays we had water from early morning until midafternoon, I decided there must be some way to put in a water heater. There was not enough current for an electric heater. One that burned wood required, not only a second flue, but a breather safety-vent on the roof for which I could not get permission. Then finally I found a butane gas heater, which the tobacconist who doubled as plumber assured me would work beautifully. There was one drawback. To be safe, to insure ventilation the glass must be removed from the bathroom window! At 2,500 feet where a normal winter offers eight months of cold and fog and snow, I thought not and so admitted defeat. After lunch on Sundays, the only time I was not apt to have callers, I "bathed" in the kitchen sink, lifting my feet up over the edge and sponging my legs as best I could with water I boiled in caldrons on the wood-burning cookstove.

Delicacies were out of the question: the procurement of the banal minimum to sustain human life required some ingenuity and a great deal of time. Butter could be purchased but long before it reached us had gone rancid in a warehouse in Bari. Salty *pecorino* cheese with an indefinable flavor of old drains and sour rags was available; *parmigiano* was not. Meat was for holidays and both tough and expensive. Fish arrived in a truck which had offered its wares to every village on its seventy-five mile route and reached us with the load reduced to a few scaley mid-sections of unknown origin and some very suspect clams which annually brought hepatitis, typhoid and most recently cholera. For an egg one made friends with a neighbor who kept chickens and then paid eight cents apiece (in 1959!). The entire stock of a grocery store could be arranged in a room the size of a closet: tinned tomatoes, tomato paste, tuna fish, anchovies, canned peas, olives, artichokes and such in oil, *pecorino*, local *salame* with intimidating cubes of fat, pasta in an amazing number of shapes and sizes, though the larger it was, the better it was liked, and a bin of bread. If you were determined, somewhere behind a counter, in a dark corner, you could find minute boxes of soap powder (though it was not in demand because dishes were still washed with sand and cinders, clothes with yellow bar soap), bottles of muriatic acid, bleach and a few tattered floor rags. All the prices were high, the quality inferior, but there was no choice. More money or less cannot improve a diet based on pasta with oil and bread with oil. Oil, which is always very important, was not a bottled, commercial product, but the local opaque syrup that both tasted good and set your teeth on edge. There was, of course, the fruit and vegetable market where greens in season were sold and fruit from Naples: three months of cauliflower and broccoli, six, it seemed, of chicory; salad in the hot months when it was most dangerous to eat. The only local fruits were cherries and figs; each has a very short season. Anything else came from outside, was pockmarked, bruised and exorbitant, the rejects of more prosperous markets sent inland.

Amusements were even more elusive. The cinema, a concrete trough like a sheep dip, was reserved to the men, as were wine shops and cafés, one of which had in its back room the only television set in town. Radio was small consolation. All stations, except those from Yugoslavia across the Adriatic, seemed to be transmitting on pendulums that bounced sounds — now clear, now faint, now clear again — off the stone cliffs of the mountains that surrounded us. One of the three Italian stations never reached us at all, not even an echo. It transmitted classical music, and we were probably considered unworthy. Few read, even those who knew how and could afford to, so the stationery and electric shop which theoretically supplied us with what we wanted, specialized in crochet instructions, and *fumetti*, the Italian adult comic books which use photographs to tell stories somewhere between soap operas and *True Confessions*.

In the evening the women had few choices. They sat, relieved if they had nothing more to do, in a vacuum between one day and the next. Sometimes they knitted coarse, heavy undershirts, sometimes they mended, badly. Those same women who used weeding hoes with infinite care and patience, lunged at their buttons and darns as though seeking revenge for the day's frustrations. All over town small groups of women, usually related one to the other by the tenuous web of their great-grandfathers' and grandmothers' marriages, sat with their feet on the half-step up to the fireplace, their shawls still around their shoulders, elbows on their knees and chins almost in the fire, murmuring the latest bits of information. They needed no newspaper. What interested them would arrive by word of mouth. They sorted the bits as they would in their season sort beans, discarding shriveled ones, putting aside the best for later consideration, spreading those to be used at the moment into a uniform mass before them. It was all done with surprising accuracy. Their elliptical comments, rooted as they were in a common past, sounded almost biblical to the outsider. When they were bored or warm enough, they went to bed. In summer the work day is longer, but the evenings are cool and soft. The caucus meets as usual, now at one's front door or on another's balcony, not out of friendship really, nor even loneliness. To them loneliness is nothing more than an arbitrary factor of life. They meet, as all cliques do, to exchange useful gossip, to laugh at the expense of others and to avoid the danger of being themselves the victims. They know that somewhere else in town they *are* the victims.

Day after day I saw these same women. At first we exchanged the usual grumblings about the weather and prices, then slowly — simply because I was always there — we began to talk of the feuds and gossip and illnesses that make up daily life, and the misery, and the frustration of change that is forever promised but never materializes. I stayed and so I shared what there was — the physical discomforts, which in time are merely irritating, and the less tangible discomforts of intuition. There is no gay cameraderie in this poverty. These are people born knowing they have no expectations. They live alone, flailing about them for some escape from impending failure, knowing that no one, not even their kin, will help them. They do not expect it. They have never had enough for themselves and cannot stop their own flailing long enough to help someone else, nor do they recognize any rule — civil, religious or emotional — that says they should. Success, should it come, will be fleeting and bring with it a few physical necessities, some envy and a spate of anonymous letters of accusation to the provincial authorities. So much depends on luck which to a peasant is an elusive power, inextricably bound up with God's will. Somehow He is not to be placated in this lifetime.

More than ten years have passed since I lived year in, year out in a southern·village, anchored there, aware each day of the disasters that plagued life and aware each day that nothing I could do was more than temporary relief. The slow repetition of those days created a sense of inner isolation that I have never entirely lost. It had nothing to do with physical distance from a more familiar world. When I went to Rome for Christmas or Easter I felt a secret joy as though I were off to an illicit love affair, not with a man, but with the comforts of a city, and like some love affairs, once I was there, I felt strangely let down. Nothing quite lived up to expectations. There was heat and light and water — all day — and rugs so deep they coddled my ankles. There were friends and parties too, at which I was driven to talk about "conditions" and petty tragedies of interest to no one, and I would suddenly realize that I had not escaped from my own isolation. I had brought it with me.

I have returned to the village frequently, but always at longer and longer intervals. When I am first there my sense of inner isolation turns outward. I am isolated from the women, they from me, though perhaps I am more aware of it because I knew them well. They never questioned my other life. For however long I stayed I was to share theirs. I came from that other world: automatically I was like the people they saw on television. They were the alienated who had nothing in common with me but their fields, their children, their troubles and finally even their jokes. Each time I go back we start again from the beginning. I must have changed. They fear that change. Some strange reversal of character may make me sneer when before I sympathized. We circle each other like stray dogs. Their features are carefully ordered to blankness. We go through the ritual of kissing on each cheek, the limp handshake and I see only a distant dull look in their eyes and deep new lines around their mouths and I think of aging. They make a careful, entirely frank inventory of me and are reassured. By comparison I have discovered the secret of eternal youth. Look at their gray hairs, their teeth falling out (which begins when they are barely children anyway), their prolapsed bellies. Why hasn't that happened to you, signora? And then their ailments. So and so has been operated on for *un male brutto*, which means cancer. *Maria u verdulaiu* died — and so we chew on the months that have passed, slowly working our way back to the present. We have begun again.

When I lived there I did not have to think each day, This is all of life, there is nothing more. I doubt that I could fight as they fight in enduring their days, or that whatever is human in me, that sets me apart from an animal, could survive their lives. They say "life brutalizes." That they recognize it explains why, for all that has been said to the contrary, they remain painfully human. They are women of tremendous strengths, these women of the shadows. One of their strengths,

9

and not the least, is their silence, which outsiders have understood as submission. I regret my own intrusion as a filter, but before they disappear to become the ghostly shadows behind a myth, I think they should have their say.

■　■　■

To go to the fields is almost a reflex,
conditioned by the absolute lack of any other
work. You go, even when you might not
have to. The donkey needs fodder: you cut
it by hand, sometimes just along the verges,
and shove it into the sacks that hang from
the saddle. While you're about it, you pull up
wild greens for a salad — a little sorrel,
dandelions, whatever there is. You weed your
patch of wheat, you loosen the dirt around
the beans, tie up a vine. You look over to see
how your neighbor's crops are coming. Not
really that you hoped yesterday's hailstorm
had beaten them down, but there would be
some justice if . . . You collect a few twigs for
kindling. And finally at some invisible cue of
light not yet changed but about to change,
the long walk back to town. Five miles, ten
— a long way with nothing to think about
except how to get a bit more land, a job —
how to feed your children. Your children.
Will they live like this? You don't ride the
donkey; he needs his strength too. The click of
his hooves, the scrape of your boots and you
almost fall asleep walking.

Together and Separate

Together, yes, at prescribed times and in prescribed places. As a woman goes to funerals with other women, and her husband with other men, so their lives seem peculiarly separate. The external rules are easy enough to understand, but there are niceties to the system that are not formal and I suspect are not discussed. Something is "right" one way and not another. For instance, if a man, whose wife I usually knew better, wanted to ask me for help or advice, his wife did not come with him, as I would have expected. He came alone. If a man I did not know wanted to see me, he brought his mother or an older woman who was a mutual acquaintance, and not as a chaperone because it was well-known that one of my neighbors had taken this chore upon herself.

The life of a normal day is strenuous, but not complex. As long as a woman is young, she and her husband share the work in the fields almost equally. The first sign of prosperity is her absence, but for now she cuts wood, digs with a mattock, weeds the grain, then ties the shocks as her husband cuts. She winnows and gleans, which he does not, and hauls sacks of grain and pitches hay. They say *rende meno* — she produces less — that is no exemption. Her help is never refused. She can drive a blindfolded mule around in circles through broad beans, while her husband turns them, or she can turn, while he drives — for endless hours in the kind of sun that makes your head throb as though some tenuous membrane between the bone and the brain itself were swelling to grotesque size and must explode. Women seldom plow or sow. Tradition and superstition are against it, although I have seen women straining at the handles of a plow to force the share as deep as possible, while their husbands dragged it back and forth across fields which suddenly seemed enormous. They are together, but they share little: sitting on a bank they eat lunch of bread and a few peppers; in the evening, another meal, usually pasta with oil or sauce, bread and perhaps some sausage, at home. What they do share is a wordless, clinging grief at the illnesses and deaths that strike their families. They never seem more helpless or closer than when they stand looking down at a mute, feverish child in a hospital bed.

Then there is the man's public world, the world of his meager pleasures from which his wife is excluded. The Piazza, the cafés, the cinema, the card games and the endless political discussions. He smokes, he drinks a little wine, he often drinks a great deal — as the women say, "What else is there for them to do?" — he may play cards, he will certainly argue with someone, and then he goes home to bed because the next morning he must go again to the fields. Besides, too many evenings have been alike.

If he owns land, it is not enough to live on; he must

rent other land or find work — and there is never enough to go around — on a construction site and leave the farming of their land mostly to his wife. Whichever way, for four winter months, he will loiter around town, trying to "play tricks on time to make it pass," avoiding, if he can, thoughts of last year or next year. His other possessions may be a two-room stone house whose roof leaks and whose chimney has smoked since man moved out of the caves, and a mule or a donkey, sometimes now even a scooter or a motorbike, a pig, a few chickens and some debts which are never quite paid before he must incur others. His clothes are simple: work trousers, boots, an old jacket, a pair of good trousers and perhaps another jacket and some black cardboard shoes with thin soles. The suit he wore at his wedding will also serve, let out and cleaned, for his burial.

A man who, with all the work he can find, never makes more than the scant minimum for survival, who, through no fault of his own, has been unable to better his sort, promise a different future to his children, improve their living quarters, or furnish enough food and clothing, can hardly be expected to feel other than inadequate and bitter. In public he is apt to cringe, not dominate. At home, where his failings are manifest, he is silent and withdrawn, only complaining with the detached but surly neutrality of a boarder about the food and the noise the children make. His rage at a thousand other things makes him snarl at the children and when, afraid that he will hit them, they cry, he takes a toothpick and his cap and disappears into the night. He may play cards or drink in the wine shops with friends as defeated as he, or he may simply stand in the Piazza until it seems probable that everyone at home has gone to bed. He knows that the food

17

is what there was, that children make noise, that his occasional brutality does not engender respect from his wife or his children, and he knows too that he cannot afford any form of amusement. Every day of his life he fights the slow corrosion of frustration. He is a man without franchise, without decisions to make or alternatives to consider. He waits through each day while the pressure of frustration builds like steam in a boiler. To survive he is almost forced to reconstruct his own ego in such a way that he can see himself as a man of power, worthy of some respect from himself and others.

Standing in the Piazza, his face unshaven, his eyes staring vacantly at some point in space, he looks mindless, but his wife would know that he was "fantasticating." It helps; though what he imagines and what did happen, all too often blur into one satisfactory event. He endows himself with power, not an easy task for someone who is apparently invisible to all men except his own kind. The most obvious power and the least easily contradicted is sexual. Now, Pancrazio's wife, didn't she look at me . . . ? From his dream to a bit of mild speculation, not really boasting yet, is a short step. His friends explore their chances in the same way, insinuating, not saying and then without noticing, they are silent again. He turns to watch a woman pass, estimates her probable charms and her husband's patent inadequacy. His attention wanders back to the day, to whatever resentment it produced. Next time I'll tell that bastard a thing or two, he promises himself. Next time. I won't let him get away with it. *He*, of course, is the *padrone*, the policeman, the tax collector, doctor, lawyer, merchant or teacher. Repetition and desire breathe life into a diatribe that never is spoken. What he will do if . . . is food for the imagination, and "Today I told him what he could do . . ." has been the preamble to thousands of fictitious conversations.

He creates a world in which he must believe because it guarantees his power and at the same time gives him something to defend, for if his sexual prowess is a threat to other men, then theirs is to him. He must assure his wife's faithfulness, his daughter's virginity, not for their sakes, for his own, for his Honor. Probably no one will ever know exactly when this cult of Honor sprang into being, but I am convinced it is a creature of the imagination. So conveniently poised between the possible and the improbable, it gives satisfaction without daily risk of proof. Think of the modern peasant, if you like, as the heir of *The Decameron*. Then he lives in a frenzy of lust and sexual activity, a threat to all women (just a look and they are aflame with passion?) and jealous of and threatened by all men. He may be, but I find it hard to believe.

Even the logistics are impossible. Overpopulation is not conducive to trysts. When husband and wife share their room, often their bed, with their children, and grandmother sleeps just the other side of the partition, it is hard to have a private fight, let alone arrange a secret meeting. On those few occasions when the street is empty, there is always an old woman peering through the crack in her "dutch" door. Empty fields do not exist. Try to take a modest sunbath and you will find out that even the trees have eyes. *Where* becomes almost unsolvable. And then there is Why. Most of us have seen the change in sexual mores, and can imagine further change, perhaps without enthusiasm, but it is conceivable. Peasants are not elastic. They are shocked by what they hear are the habits of the young in cities (at least now they hear) and cling to a strict, almost Victorian code. A man and a woman must never be left alone together, or the worst will happen. Men have terrible, overwhelming physical needs; women must grin and bear it. Peasant women seldom see physical encounters as pleasant. As something necessary, as duty, as trial but not passion, which is a word associated with rage rather than love or sexual intercourse.

I have heard more than one woman regret the end of the government-run houses of prostitution, and I have seen the long lines of peasant men, standing in a side Piazza, waiting to get into the House for their five minutes. ("Time's up!" and over the partition comes a roll of toilet paper.) A squalid, melancholy little scene which was repeated every Saturday and Sunday evening for years. Where, then, were all those panting maidens and passionate wives who yearned for the attentions of these men? There is no way to avoid it: peasant women are not universally plagued by irresistible fiery longings, but the men need to think so, and the women let them. Men have been much more cruelly deceived. Peasant women are by instinct pragmatic enough to let the illusion stand: they may even sense its importance to men who have nothing else. When they are alone, talking, a wife who boasts of her husband's sexual charms always says the same thing with wan pride: "He's *valente, valente!*" He's very, very quick.

So the man dawdles in the Piazza, fantasticating, almost imagining himself what he is not. His frustration is always there, like a corn, pinching him, but never quite driving him to act. He is unsure of his rights or even his rightful expectations and too diffident to do more than resent. But, occasionally, if it is very hot and especially at the time of the *festa*, when the harvest is in, when he must admit once more that he has too little to get through the winter, when the cost of shoes and sweaters and trousers for his family has frightened him and when he has had enough wine, his frustrations and resentments combine in a moment of mad thrashing protest. Snubs that were not snubs and idle comments that he only half heard and half interpreted through the haze of his twilight daydreams come back to him. Then one remark, one not even intended for him, will send him lunging into a fight. To outsiders it seems a sudden animal attack without provocation. His rage is never directed at the real causes of his bitterness — that he would not quite dare — but at another peasant whom he loathes in the sneering, picking way of people who are born together and are apt to die together.

There is release in violence, no matter how futile the motive. An argument is a purge. He can rage at home and rant in public and for once he has in his grasp something he can manage. What should be at most a pointless feud can (and now and then does) become a knife slashing or worse, a murder. Barbaric, immoral, illegal? Certainly. Man is, at times, all these things, but it is also an involuntary catharsis that man resorts to when poverty, boredom and frustration overload his reason. (In recent years we have seen the poor in large cities all over the world react with the same kind of explosive aggression.) Hot blood, or that much-vaunted Latin temperament are credited, half-proudly, with being the cause, as though they excuse anything, but if the Southern Italian peasant were so hot-blooded, hundreds of years ago he would have murdered the petty tyrants and bigoted provincial clergy who have made his life a Golgotha. Instead he stands in the Piazza, brooding and resentful. Torn between the misty pleasures of imagination and the obvious dangers of action, he forces his own defeat upon himself.

To a woman each day is a many-headed monster. Her approach to it varies, not simply because she is different from any other woman, but because custom, which orders so much of visible life, changes from district to district, even from town to town. History, climate, the crops raised and the kind of labor they require can explain many of the disparities; others are mysterious remnants of usages that have outlived their origins. Why, for instance, do the women in one village compete to see which of them can "keep her husband in the Piazza" with good clothes on his back and money in his pockets? And who in highest style? The men are drones, publicly on show to prove their wives' superiority. Why are the women of one village famous witches, of another skillful midwives? Why are women forbidden to carry water in just one village?

In certain parts of Sicily young peasant women live in an Italian purdah. They should never be in their houses alone and are usually watched over by their Hecatean mothers-in-law. They may scuttle through the back streets, avoiding the Corso and the Piazza, to the market just before daybreak or just at dark, and then probably not alone. In the end they give up and send their children trotting off in relays to the grocer and the shoemaker and the fruit vendor.

The wide fertile plains of Puglia are studded with towns where from 30,000 to 100,000 people appear to be camping in the ruins of some recent earthquake.

These agglomerations claim to be cities and to prove it can show the requisite number of low "skyscrapers" and polished aluminum show windows in shops which are now, suddenly, "boutiques." Still, 80 percent of the inhabitants are farm workers and peasants. They live in sprawling warrens of one-room houses with the usual allotment of donkeys, mules, carts, chickens, pigs, rabbits, dogs, cats and children. Some of the alley-streets have fragments of paving that connect a network of wandering troughs and potholes; others are more honestly posted *"Non transitabile."* For twenty years the installation of sewers or water pipes or light lines have been the excuses for this chronic disorder. Each doorway is draped with plastic strips to keep out flies. There a peasant woman works in the fields when she can, especially in the rush of various harvests, but her first duty is to contend with the complexities normal to any city. She spends half her life standing in lines, waiting to pay bills or apply for certificates (for instance, each child who goes to school needs ten to be admitted). If she can find paid work, so much the better. Still she must shop, cook, try to find water enough to wash the dishes and the dirty clothes. Gone are the days when the entire family, the women in flowing white muslin albs, climbed into the high-wheeled cart and drove to the sea and beyond, right into the water for their weekly scrub. The winter muck of too many people, too many animals becomes the spring playground of flies and rats. Soon baby Giovanni is feverish and five-year-old Mario is in shock from diarrhea. The plagues, which for centuries have been endemic, return to test the survival powers of the unfit and the women rush from doctor to saint to sorcerer for potions against the evil eye and on to a miraculous Madonna. Always they are one step behind disaster, trying in their desperation to lay it low with the blunt instruments of superstition.

The two regions I know best, the Abruzzo and Lucania, are bare and mountainous, with villages, some very large, perched precariously on high slopes or even cloudy little pinnacles, where, generations ago, it was decided they could best defend themselves from the invaders and malaria of the valleys below. The fields are no larger than two or three sheets spread out, a saddle here, a patch there. Machinery is of little use and would only turn up more rocks and clay. Long since the topsoil has been washed out to sea by torrential rains, and that man still persists says much for his secret powers of optimism and more for his determination to live. Few things are certain, but, as is the way in such places, those that are work together with ruinous cooperation. The only abundance is the weather, which with perfect inverted timing stunts the crops that would keep man alive another year. Wind singes the olives. Rain uproots seedlings. Hail strafes ripe wheat. Grapes must swell in searing heat.

The men and women who do resist were born there. They must all find work: there is never enough. A few have given up and simply wait to be rescued by some new government subsidy. Peasant women know they must do whatever needs to be done, and there is so much more than just their work in the fields. They string tomatoes and peppers, cure olives in brine, pack the relish they use all winter in oil, help slaughter the pigs they have raised and then chop them into a million cubes for sausage. Even now many of them make their own bread in large round loaves because its heavy sogginess is more filling than the baker's product. They cook and launder. If they come by a fertile postage stamp of land near the point where the main sewer surfaces into an open ditch, they plant a vegetable garden and sell their produce in the market. They even serve as mules when there are none. They have babies, gaggles of them, who need to be nursed, swaddled and disciplined in the brutal loving ways only harassed mothers can invent. And as though their days were not busy enough, they cannot reject *any* work for which money is offered, except actual prostitution.

(There are, however, prostitutes. Sometimes when I ran nurseries they seemed to be my most loyal supporters, producing as they did a variegated array of babies at regular intervals. Unfortunately contraception remains an esoteric mystery to the two or three self-proclaimed whores each village supports. The first and most tragic one I ever knew lived in the hedges outside town, waiting for men on their way to or from the wine shops. She charged fifty *lire* (eight cents). She knew no other way to make a living. During the war her entire family had been killed in the shelling of the town, and she, to stay alive, started swapping favors for bread. By the time I knew her she had three scrawny, yellowish children with huge eyes and pinched little faces for whom she asked places each year at the nursery. We could not take them because she was both tubercular and syphilitic. Another who flourished in the trade, at much higher fees, forgot to feed her little boy, Tommaso, for days on end. She had tricked the local authorities into assigning an apartment to her in a public housing project. It was completely bare except for two pieces of professional equipment: an umbrella and a bed. Tommaso was so entranced by the permanent audience he found at the nursery that all the words dammed up in his little mind during the lonely months he had wandered the alleys and courtyards came pouring out. We had assumed that when his mother was out or not "busy," he slept in her bed. Only after several

25

weeks of his hilarious and tragic stories of what "last night's bridegroom" (*lo sposo d'ieri sera*) as he invariably called them, had said and done, did we realize that he slept quietly *under* the bed.)

For most women such adventures are the material of gossip: the work for which *they* are paid is the common drudgery of every village — day work in the fields which they hate; cutting and hauling wood; the shopping, cooking and cleaning for a "Signora"; swabbing down stairs and hallways; carrying bulbous, two-kilo loaves of bread, five or six to a load, on planks balanced on their heads from the baker's to the various storekeepers; unloading sacks of salt, feed and fertilizer from trucks; and *in extremis* as masons' helpers, carrying hods of mortar to him and hods of rubble away to the dump. As their lives are arranged and have been for centuries, peasants have only one absolute responsibility — the family.

The women earn the most dependable supply of cash. They help with all the crops, raise as many small animals as they can find space and feed for and then market them with acumen. Somehow they are the ones who understand the intricacies of local bureaucracy and politics, so they sense who can be tricked, forced or cajoled into granting a subsidy, a house, a sack of flour. They teach their children, and it is often the soundest teaching they will receive, right from wrong, the "proper" ways of the community and the few skills they possess. Ultimately they decide on the size of their daughters' dowries and then collect the linens piece by piece, for they are the ones who actually control the purse and decide what purchases shall be made each week in the market. Most important of all, these women create security for their children which no spanking or screaming rage will ever undermine. Each has nursed her child, fondled him, rocked him to sleep and cared for him when he was sick until he knows his mother loves him, not in exchange for good behavior or a chore done, but simply because she loves him. He is hers. She is to her children, as the Madonna is to the believing Catholic of her society, all-forgiving, all-protecting. This is the aim of most mothers, but they seldom carry the weight of total responsibility. The comparison could be carried still further, though it is hard to know whether the practices of the Catholic Church in Southern Italy are the result of a domestic evolution of theology or simply versatile adaption to the mores of the parish. The Marian cult exists and has become the core of local belief. The apparitions of the Virgin Mary escape any attempt to catalogue them, much less verify them, but that makes no more difference than the rosy stupidity of the modern plaster statues. Mary, the Earth-Mother figure, can be loved, trusted and prayed to, while God and His son, Jesus, remain cold symbols. The Holy Ghost, so elusive anyway, is quite literally the white plaster bird that hovers uncertainly over all altars. Men find it hard to be humble before other men, even harder to lose face, so praying to a woman for her intercession is less abrasive to the ego. Women can identify immediately with the all-suffering Mother and perhaps take consolation in her importance to all men. Much as the Vatican may deplore it, in the South Christ is on the altar, but the people pray to and worship the Virgin Mary.

The women, as they grow older and their children marry, struggle less. They know they will be taken care of. In many ways theirs have been and continue to be surrogate lives. They have snatched power without appearing to and reap happiness from the uncritical devotion of their children, most especially their sons.

27

Strangely, they still have the courage to attack when their sons hesitate. He looks for an excuse to avoid definite action: she looks forward to victory. Much has changed in the last twenty years. Industrialization and life in the cities that spawn it are too sophisticated for peasant women. Their sons escape into a world they do not know, to earn and then spend inconceivable amounts of money. Mothers' influence is yearly less, but it almost seems that their daughters and daughters-in-law may have learned their lessons well, for now they are more demanding — of money, clothes, attention and help.

At home in Lucania change is still suspect and slow to come. As before, women carry much of the burden and claim the power they earn in devious ways that will be slow a-dying, for women, once they are sure they can manage the problems of their days, are unwilling to abdicate to men who have never known that confidence. Alone, the decisions are theirs. They farm the land, sell what they judge should be sold and blackmail the authorities into supplying what they feel is their right. Their husbands will be very conservative about the use of any money left over from what they have sent home: it should be spent for new stoves, hot water heaters, if they live in public housing apartments, for shiny marble-chip floors to replace bricks or for outside plaster, if they own a small house. Like land, a house is "real" and will always have a value. The women may be less cautious. I have known some who became entrepreneurs in a small way, buying bits of land and hiring men to work it at day wages. One of their great pleasures is being able to fire the men and replace them with others more willing to work. If the land has never attracted, and some have been too bitter to admit it ever did, they start small stores and hope to expand. They will, like crabgrass.

These are not lovable women. They are blunt, often crude and at times unable to control their grotesque ferocity. Their minds are not cluttered by theories; they know no extenuating circumstances; almost any means, except murder, can be justified. They watch others prosper in the eternal treasure hunt, while they fall behind, mystified by the clues that seem anagrams half-solved. Their salvation is and has been that they have always known the secrets of their own world and how to use them, sometimes in wondrously subtle ways. And they have never been afraid to work. To say that 7.2 women out of every 10 buy .9 of a dress a year, while 6.7 of 10 buy 5.8 pairs of shorts for their husbands, says nothing about them. I have not even tried to calculate what they buy, how often their husbands beat them, or how often they have sexual intercourse. I know them as Teresa who solves problems this way, Maria that way, and Carmela, with whom everyone can work because no matter what the tension she has a remark ready to ease it. They have a certain wit and resourcefulness and a kind of bludgeoning courage. If and when they are compassionate with each other, they never relax so far that they cannot still hear that little voice whispering, "Watch out! She needs you now, but later . . ."

It goes without saying that their loyalty to their own is unshakable.

The women know how to sign their own names, but in any practical sense they are illiterate. Fortunately they have encyclopedic memories. I asked Chichella once how they could remember everything, dates, names, what places looked like and what people said. She gave me a little half-smile, not of self-pity, but of apology and said: "That's all we have." They were willing to share it.

Not even water is easily come by — houses
in the old quarter still do not have it. The
aqueduct runs three, maybe four hours a day,
and then, as though to remind you that
cleanliness is next to godliness, all Saturday
night and much of Sunday. Families that
leave for the fields before dawn, return at
dusk to find there is no water. Like most
others, water is a woman's task. Each knows
where there is a fountain that leaks an
invisible thread or a spring that oozes up
through mud and rocks. It may be a two-mile,
a three-mile walk, but without water . . .
She takes her knitting and the bucket and
plods slowly out and even more slowly
back home.

Peppina

For several years I shared my landing with a short, lumpy woman named Peppina, who at the first sound of a footstep on the stairs, came to her door, always with a baby sucking at a breast, and looked out. She appeared to be dressed in hand-me-downs, clean and neatly darned, but definitely intended for a taller, slighter figure. Sweaters pulled across her bosom and crept higher and higher above the waist, while zippers took on a life of their own, slithering down almost as soon as she had modestly pulled them up. Her preoccupation with callers must have been nothing more than a conditioned reflex because she had few herself and was so little the meddler that, when she realized it was someone to see me, she ducked back into her apartment and silently closed the door. Another, as I had reason to know, would have stood, listening to any conversation as though authorized by divine right. Later Peppina would knock on my door and apologize.

She was a cheerful woman who smiled often, revealing a sad collection of small, very white, alternate teeth. Her light green eyes always looked exhausted. She had every reason to be. In the fifteen years I have known her there have been only brief periods when she was not either nursing a baby or pregnant. Then she appeared to be about forty: instead she was twenty-five. She already had three children, the baby and two toddlers of identical size with enormous brown eyes who lingered in perpetuity on the stairs. Living so close together we could hardly avoid knowing more and more about each other.

Her husband, Minguccio (a nickname for Domenico), worked in Germany as a construction carpenter. Her mother lived with her and the children because, as she explained, she had five brothers, all either in the North or in Germany, and their wives made no secret of how difficult they found their mother-in-law. She had struggled to raise her sons, worked to feed them and now expected to rule in their households. She was not happy living with Peppina simply because Peppina was her *daughter:* she expected the full attention of her sons. They, I am sure, were relieved to escape, for she was a real crone, fat, stone deaf, quarrelsome with everyone and devoted to alcohol, brandy by preference but wine if there was nothing better. She was also a glutton. If I were cooking anything that smelled good, I could expect a knock on the door. It would be mother. "What are you having for dinner?" And when I told her, "Can I have some?" Peppina would arrive to take her away, returning to apologize, always in the same way. "Be patient, she's old." For short periods mother would disappear and I knew that a son had returned, but soon enough she would be back.

For all that Peppina was cheerful, she seemed to struggle under the weight of some lifelong sadness. Her voice was subdued — which is not to say she could not screech with the best of them when she felt like it — and even her walk was deliberate as though arriving a minute sooner or a minute later could change nothing. How often I have seen her, sitting with a child in her arms and her head propped against the glass of her balcony door, gazing out blindly, and wondered what thoughts could bring such desolation to her face. If she were going to talk about herself, she always shrugged and began, "What can you expect? *Nothing!*" Then she would stop, and each time I thought she would not go on but usually she did.

"You probably can't believe it, but I was pretty once, not just when I was little, but later too, when I grew up, when Minguccio asked to marry me. Then I was still pretty. Didn't have all this belly," and she pounded her stomach in irritation. "I don't remember much about my father, but before he went to Africa — he said he was going to win the war and we'd all go there and have land, but then he was killed and we stayed right here — but before that the men at the *masseria* teased him, I can remember it. He'd bounce me up and down on his knee and they'd say 'You wait and see what trouble she's going to cause you. Just you wait! When you get back, won't be any way to keep the boys away from her!' I was little then, and he didn't come back. He was a shepherd for one of the old landowners — he's dead now too. His sons weren't interested in the land. They all went to Naples and never came back. I don't even remember them. My father? Yes, he was permanent out there. They gave us a room to live in and some ground Mamma could work, and there were the other men too who made their deals year to year, and their families lived there too. When I was little, I liked it. There were always lots of children around and we had chores, sure, but we had fun too. Nobody worried about sending us to school, particularly us girls. After my father went to the war, they let mamma stay on — my brother Tommaso was fourteen by then and he kept the sheep and Mamma worked in the fields, and they let us stay.

"Then once we knew my father was dead, the other women out there started saying Mamma was after their husbands — it wasn't true, but that's what they said and besides they thought she and Tommaso, together, didn't do as much as a man could do. They had some relatives, see, who were looking for a place, so they said Mamma was no better than a whore. That's when we moved to town. It was a bad time after the war. Mamma's pension never came. 'Just wait, Zi' Rosa, it'll come,' they'd tell her at the post office, but it never did until five or six years ago and then not all of it. We didn't know anybody, like some of the others, to push it. We had to take what came — when it came. So Mamma worked at anything she could get and that's why she's so old now. Not that she is, I mean that's why she seems so old and that's why I try to be patient with her. She worked — God alone knows how hard — and the only advice she ever gave me was 'Face it! You're going to work all your life, but don't ever work in the fields — no matter how hungry you are, no matter what they offer you. Don't ever start, or they won't let you off till you're half dead and good for nothing else.' She never stopped to think that was all I knew how to do.

"Oh sure, I worked in the fields — that's how I got to know Minguccio. He took some land — regular sharecropping deal — and farmed it, and going back and forth to the fields I used to meet him on the road and we'd walk together. He hoped he'd get land from the Land Reform, but he never did . . . and he had three bad years in a row where he could hardly pay what he owed, so he gave up and started construction work — there was more of it then. Still, he's never lost the urge to farm. He'd do it now if he could make it — but you can't make it if you don't own anything. Well, then we got married, and he said, No more work in the fields, but I still did a lot of the time, especially when he didn't have work. Like I told him, we couldn't starve just because of his pride, so I'd go out by the day — for good pay. After the baby was born though, I never got my strength back right, so I promised to give it up. Like I said, what can you expect?"

By the time I knew her Peppina did any work she could find, usually cleaning hallways. She also had a permanent, but very loose arrangement with a doctor's wife who lived nearby, that she would come in whenever needed which, in practice, meant that she always did the morning shopping, the hauling of water, the lunch dishes and sometimes the cooking. Unfortunately all the work she found was on the basis of a favor; even the doctor's wife paid her at irregular intervals, and then whatever came into her mind as fair. Remittances from Germany varied according to how much work Minguccio had been able to find. Some years were good, others bad, and too, his only skill required in mild weather. There have been months when Peppina, her mother and the children lived on garlic pizza, a slab of leavened dough covered with slices of garlic and olive oil and then baked for 20 *lire* (3 cents) in the baker's oven.

One night several months after Peppina had moved next to me, my butane gas ran out, as it always seems to, right in the middle of boiling pasta, and I rushed, pot in hand, across the landing to ask if I might finish cooking it on her stove. When she opened the door, I noticed that her usual high color had given way to a waxy pallor, and she was reluctant to let me in, would not, in fact, let me by with my pot. She stood firmly in the doorway, stuttering disconnected words from which I gathered only that I was not welcome. As I started to turn away, she stopped me, then sighed deeply as though resigned to some awful punishment.

"Give it to me. I'll take it downstairs to what's-her-name." I knew she was flustered and that only the nickname had come to her mind. "When it's ready, I'll bring it up to you." And she shuffled off down the stairs.

While I waited, half of my mind wondering about Peppina, the other half busy with the last minute preparations, for pasta is a very short-order sort of dish, it came to me: Peppina was without gas too, probably because she had no money to pay for a new "bomb." Several minutes later she came back with my pot, forked the spaghetti out onto a plate, put sauce, then cheese, then more sauce on it and motioned me to the table. She sat down opposite me and commented, "It's warm in here." I looked at her face and saw that her cheeks were once more bright pink. As I remember it, all I saw was, "What's the matter?" The story came spilling out with some quiet tears of relief. All those months she must have felt terribly alone, but there had always been a smile.

In August when Minguccio had last been home, he bought new kitchen furniture. Indeed, her cupboards were brown and white formica and there was a formica table with spindly chrome legs and chairs to match which already had a tendency to wobble. Before he bought them, he had sat at the old table with his money in front of him and done the calculations over and over again, she said. He needed a certain amount for the trip, for one month's room and board in case he could not have his job back immediately, then he allowed a monthly sum for his family — she did not tell me how much, though I imagine it took into account her earnings — and decided there was enough left for the furniture. Peppina had not really cared about it. She wanted a real stove with an oven to replace the two-burner gas ring, but had hesitated to say so because, as she explained, he had little enough satisfaction from his work and little enough time he could be at home. If he wanted the furniture first, then the stove would come next. She was not willing to give in about the stove another time. Minguccio wanted a dining room set that would sit, shiny and unused, in the small front room.

Peppina said, "That's for people with money. We eat in the kitchen at the kitchen table and we always will, so the stove's the important thing."

After her husband had left, she found an extra job cutting and hauling wood and she began to worry again about the stove. She knew that prices always went up around Christmas. If she could buy it before, she would save. She counted and recounted what was owed to her and what she could expect to earn in those months. (No matter how little schooling they may have had, the women are experts at "doing sums" on their fingers.) In the end she was sure: she signed the time notes, paid the first and the second. Everything was all right. Then there had been a cable from Minguccio. He was sick, the usual winter flu, and needed money to pay his expenses until he could work again. So her troubles had begun and with each day worsened. She owed the grocer so much now that he would not give her more credit. The next to last note was almost due on the stove. She had no wood and finally, a few days before, no more gas. She was running out of flour and soon would not even be able to make garlic pizza. The doctor's wife had not paid her, neither had the man for whom she had cut wood. She had fed the family on what she earned scrubbing hallways: 2,000 *lire* a month for each one — she cleaned two — they were living on $6.60 a month. Somehow the children had to eat and stay warm. She dreaded losing her equity in the stove and almost more, the unpaid note on her record, for it would be sent to the bank for collection and eventually to the courts, if she did not pay. And still she could not bring herself to insist with the people who owed her money for work she had already done.

"No, no, I can't go to them. I can't. You know how they are. If I go and complain that I need the money — let's say they pay me — but next time they'll find someone else to do the work, someone who waits. I've tried to find more work. There isn't any. If I lose what I have, I'll never get any more. No, I can't ask them." And she was not asking me: she was explaining why she had acted strangely at her door. I asked if she had paid the rent and then remembered her mother's pension.

"Eh — who pays rent here? No one! The government owns these buildings and everybody says why should we pay anything to them. They owe us more than we'll ever get. My trouble is I sublet — from my cousin — but he knows I'll pay and after all it's not costing him anything. As for Mamma and her pension, you can forget that. It all goes in her postal savings book — to bury her, she says. She wants what she calls a 'good funeral' with the bells ringing and the black carriage out. I haven't even asked her. One of my brothers might get some of it out of her, if he was in real trouble, but she wouldn't give me any, even if I was dying. Once before I asked her. I'm not going to give her the pleasure of turning me down another time. Forget her and her pension."

Her instinct, for which she paid dearly, was never to offend anyone. Mine was not to lend money, but that night I did. We drew up a note between us, that is I wrote it and after she had practiced her signature several times, she signed it. I gave her the exact sum of the two final payments on the stove (less than $30) with two stipulations: she was to tell *no one*, not even Minguccio, and she must not pay me back until after Christmas, when he had already returned to Germany. He need never know. I suggested that she pay the note due now and put the rest down against her bill at the grocer's. Before the final note came up, someone would surely pay her, I argued (and hoped). She nodded slowly, her eyes wide and no longer dulled with worry.

"No one?" she asked.

"No one, and I mean no one! I cannot lend money. If I do, everyone in town will be at the door."

Her head continued to bobble back and forth like a toy dog's. I knew she was thinking, convincing herself that I meant what I said. In the end she must have, for no one, not even her husband, has ever known about our arrangement.

When I had finished my supper, she insisted on washing the dishes (water from the Sitz bath, boiled on the neighbor's stove, etc.), and I realized she intended to be a resident handmaiden for any chores. As hard as I tried, I never convinced her she owed me *no* service. "If it's my pleasure," she would say and go right on doing it. That night as she left I made her take some wood: the next day I ordered new gas bombs for us both.

Some weeks later Minguccio came home for Christmas, looking gaunt and pale. He was a slight man with a long thin nose that accentuated the boniness of his face and small dark eyes, which, though they darted to attention at the slightest movement, were neither frightened nor scheming. He was an extremely quiet man, courteous but always alert, in case the friend of yesterday had become the enemy to watch today. His first night home, he came to call without Peppina. This was the first of dozens of such visits, always the night he arrived and the night before he left. Apparently my sitting room made him nervous for he never paused, but went straight to the kitchen where he sat on a chair, gazing between his knees at the floor. He never accepted anything except a cup of coffee which he drank while he smoked a cigarette. The first time he wanted to thank me. He understood I had been very kind to his wife and children. When I looked surprised, he said, "Oh, and she told me that we owe you wood. I'll replace it tomorrow. She says she has paid you for the gas 'bomb.' She did, didn't she?" He only wanted my confirmation. "You say it is not very much, but if you are without wood and gas, and *worse*, without money, you are without your whole world. We thank you. We will not impose on your kindness."

His phrases were always stilted — whether from shyness or an innate mental precision, I have never known. All of our conversations have had an almost Chinese formality about them and yet over the years I have come to know him well. He told me once that his life in Germany was easier for him than for the others because he did not sit worrying every night about what his wife

42

might have found to do. "She is a good woman, and I know she is faithful to me. The others — not one of them is sure. It brings on a kind of madness."

In those early years, after he had finished his day's work, he was the cook of the barracks in which some twenty Italian men lived. He had not wanted to be, but he had recognized that they were all wasting money cooking their individual dinners on the gas rings and had suggested a communal fund for the shopping and a planned meal that suited them all. Everyone had agreed and of course elected him to do the work. Later a family that ran a café let him sleep in a room above their garage in exchange for work several hours each evening. They learned to trust him. He was proud when they asked him to take dinner with them on Sundays; one summer he did not return to Italy at all, but stayed in Germany tending the café while the family took a vacation. After some ten years there he had found a contractor who hired him year round, still allowing the required visits to Italy, and a family who gave him a room of his own, and even toward the end, I believe, all his evening meals. Germany was never home to him, he did not like it, but he had made the best he could of it, and in return had the consolation of some comfort and trust.

Through those years our visits continued, even after Peppina had arranged, in some mysterious way she was never willing to discuss, for an apartment in a public housing unit to be assigned directly to them and so avoided the expense of subletting. Now they lived a hundred yards from me and though I saw her constantly, there was no longer the intimacy of the shared landing. One summer I saw the children, now five of them, dressed in the most fragile white summer suits and matching white shoes. At his next visit Minguccio reported that "it had been decided" all money should be managed by Peppina and I imagined her scowl of disapproval at those extravagant clothes. They were saving for a television set, another of Peppina's ideas, to keep the children at home now they were of what she called "the wandering age" and too, although she did not admit it, because the evenings were long and dreary sitting with her mother. Most of the time they had enough to eat, enough wood and even a few extra clothes, but at the cost of so many hard days and lonely nights.

Peppina lost a few more teeth and gained a few more pounds and still looked tired. Had all her pregnancies gone full term, her rapid decay into precocious middle age would have been even more exaggerated. She never talked about it. I think she assumes that I know, for procured abortion is the only reasonable explanation for her sudden miscarriages. They have never happened when Minguccio was at home. I do not think he has the slightest suspicion. Each time there was enough food prepared to feed the children for several days, the laundry had just been done, and she had warned the doctor's wife she would be unable to work. With the preparations in order, she walked into town as she did every morning, stayed late, came home and took to her bed. Three days later, pale and a trifle unsteady, she reappeared and picked up her life where she left off. She worries, sometimes out loud, because she cannot go to confession. There can be no other reason: five children were not born. Her Church says she murdered them. There should be twelve, instead of seven, and I am sure the seventh would not be alive had Minguccio not been home all of one winter.

At Christmas he came back sick "in his intestines," Peppina said, and went to the hospital for x-rays. The

44

adventures of anyone brave enough to enter the town hospital are a story in themselves: it was always impossible to diagnose or cure anyone there and so it became a place to die. A specialist comes twice a week to read x-rays, but again the result is inevitable: the films are not clear. The patient will have to go to Bari, or Potenza, or Salerno, and have them redone. Minguccio traveled up and down the provinces following each doctor's recommendations with little success. Peppina said he had bouts of fever, but he had always been a man who stayed at home, so it was hard to tell when he was sick and when he felt better. On sunny afternoons I would see him, thinner than ever, and pale, walking along the road with the three youngest children. When he was with them, he always smiled.

Peppina, I knew, was gone most of the day. She had found two other families for whom to work. At first she had staggered back from the Piazza, carrying her own shopping, the doctor's wife's, and that of the two new families, then she forced her eldest daughter, Rosa, to go with her and carry half the burden. Rosa resented it. On their way back they always met her friends ambling to school, and she was ashamed that she had to work before she could join them. One morning Peppina, who had ignored the bridling and complaints, lost her temper and beat the girl in the middle of the road where everyone could see and hear.

"You're ashamed, are you?" she screamed. "I'll give you something to be ashamed of," and she slapped her in the head once. She stood back and watched Rosa cry and when she had almost stopped, Peppina slapped her again and again. "There! Now get moving. We're going home." And the little girl came howling behind her.

For several days Rosa went around with a swollen

face and was silent in a sullen, caged animal way. "That's the trouble with the schools," Peppina told me. "They make them think they are too good for work." After that Rosa did one hallway while her mother did the other, but they alternated so that Peppina could be sure her daughter was doing her work properly. Then they went to the market. That winter Rosa learned what her mother considers a Commandment: there is no escape from work.

When it was time to leave for Germany, Minguccio stayed at home. Peppina worked and the gloom of winter settled upon them. Early in April she told me she was pregnant and added: "This time there's nothing to do about it." Slowly she began to swell, but she worked every day. Minguccio was better that spring. One day he asked to borrow money for cigarettes until Peppina came home. She carried all their money with her. "She's good at managing it, you know," he said with no sign of hurt pride. "And she knows what we need." In May he found a job as a construction worker on a new road, not as a carpenter, just as a manual laborer, but he seemed to think he could make it at home. Perhaps the days of Germany were over for good.

Summer is always easier. With the sun hope returns and nothing is totally impossible. But the weather was against Minguccio. Although there would have been more work on the road, in late September torrents of rain brought landslides, followed by fog and finally snow. For two months not a shovel was moved. Minguccio was at home, keeping the fire. Peppina worked more and more slowly.

Maria was born in mid-December 1971. I happened to be there visiting. She was the seventh child, the fourth girl. Peppina was thirty-eight. I saw her just once at home in her own bed where she had given birth to all of her children, helped by the midwife and her husband's sister. This had been a long, exhausting labor. She worried because she was so weak. She said only one thing that was at all extraordinary for such visits. She told me that her husband's family was mad at her. Her own no longer existed: her mother had died in the spring, her brothers were still in the North or in Germany.

"If I do what I have to do, tell them there is no shame in making a living. Shame is in living off others."

Later I understood.

That Easter she waited until everyone had gone to Mass and then came across the courtyard to see me, to explain what she had done, almost as though she had to excuse herself to me. I was amused when she started off, as always.

"What can you expect? *Nothing!*" And she paused. "Do you remember when I told you that day I had to do what I had to do? You've probably heard about it. It'd be too good to keep, no? But see it was our only chance, or it seemed like it. There wasn't any work here. Minguccio didn't get better really, partly because he's discouraged — that may have been the disease. Sometimes I think it is, except I don't say that to him.

"Well, anyway, before you came to see me that time, I'd found out that an army officer and his wife in Rome — his brother works in Bari, that's how I found out about it — they were looking for a wet-nurse for their baby. The people who told me about it kept saying — 'It's light work, Peppina. The important thing is you've got to be clean and healthy. Really clean!' Well, nobody's ever accused me of being dirty — shapeless maybe and I'm no princess, even when I get done up in my best clothes — but I'm not dirty. The doctor's certificate said I was healthy, didn't have any of some funny-sounding diseases he wrote down. When I saw you that time, I'd already decided. I was going to do it even if Minguccio got mad. He'd be busy enough taking care of the children. You see, they said they'd pay me 180,000 *lire* a month ($289), and if everything worked out right, they'd try to find a job for Minguccio too. What can you expect?" This time she paused, but never gave her stock answer. "I believed them. I left New Year's day — it was awful. Even Minguccio cried when I got on the bus and I thought I can't stand this, but we went on — I had the baby with me and Benito — poor little thing, he got so tired on the trip. (He was eighteen months old.) When we took the train in the morning it was still dark and we never got there until almost dinner time and it was dark again. We wouldn't have lived through the trip either, if people hadn't been nice and taken Benito for walks in the corridor and shown him what was outside the window and things.

"They were there, all right, at the station to meet us. He wasn't so bad, making jokes and tickling Maria and all. He had a little moustache and he was sort of stocky, not fat, but he looked like he was stuffed into his uniform and the buttons might begin to pop any minute. Funniest thing about him was he carried his lunch to the office in a leather briefcase, like a workman, just so he could avoid spending money. But her — when I saw her, I knew she was going to be trouble. All fox-faced and mincing and calling him 'Titti' like she was a little girl, begging from her daddy.

"I don't know even now where we went. Everything looked the same to me — those modern buildings, one after another, one after another, like celery in a field. This one had an elevator. I thought I was going to be sick before it stopped — later I got used to it. Then she says to me — 'Right in here. You're to sleep with the two babies.' *Two babies!* Turned out they were the two youngest, but there were four, and I had to take care of them. Nurse the little baby, take care of the little boy, he was three or four months older than Benito, and the two older ones. I had to take them to school every morning, pick them up at lunchtime and keep after them the rest of the day too. Ooh, signora! The first morning I took them to school I got lost going back and no one could understand me when I asked for the Colonel's street. I said it as clear as I could, the way I'd understood it, but they just looked at me like I was crazy. Suddenly I turned a corner and there she was! The signora in her bathrobe with a coat over it. She started screaming at me. She wasn't paying big wages to have me see the sights of Rome, and where'd I been and what did I think I was doing? Oh, on and on she went. Like Rosaria — that was the maid and she was almost as old as Mamma and as tired — like Rosaria always said, *'Quella carogna'* — That slut! — Excuse the expression, but that's what she was. *Una carogna,* and I knew it from the first day when she started on about the milking machine, like what they use on cows, that's what she said I had to do. I was a wet-nurse, but the baby got his milk from a bottle! She wouldn't let me give him my breast — no, oh no! He had to have it from a bottle — a boiled bottle! Why'd she need me, then? Well, I can tell you that too, in a minute. The milking machine hurt. I tried to reason with her. Why couldn't I wash the tit in alcohol, just the way I did for the machine, then if she thought I'd infect the baby, I'd use a plastic shield, but let the baby suck like a real baby. No, no and no! The milking machine! Pretty soon I had sores and everytime I had to use the machine they'd open and hurt and I'd sit there crying, wondering why Jesus let me do it. Then I'd think about the alternatives and just go on. There weren't any. And the pay was good.

"Poor old Rosaria. I was about dead keeping up with six children — and I did all their laundry too — but to help Rosaria I said I'd iron the Colonel's shirts. Then we decided the best way was to do all the laundry at once, so I did it and I did all the ironing. Poor Rosaria. We'd talk while we worked. She was a widow. There was a long story about her husband. He'd been a drunk, but finally he fell and hurt himself and died. She said it was the only good thing he'd done in thirty years. The trouble was some of the stamps for his pension weren't paid up, or something like that, so the insurance still wasn't paying her anything. 'Otherwise I'd shake this *carogna*,' she'd say and laugh. At night we did the dishes together and then sat and talked when we weren't too tired. The cleaning and the cooking, all those meals — it was just too much for her. So one morning I'm nursing Maria. It was early, but I'd already done little Giancarlo's ration — with the machine — *sissignora* — when fox-face comes in and says like she's commenting on the weather, 'I've sent Rosaria away. She's not up to doing what we want, but I'm sure you can, Peppina. You get everything done so fast, a little extra cooking won't bother you.' I wanted to tell her what she could do with that, but I kept repeating to myself 180,000, 180,000, 180,000 a month, Peppina don't say it. Don't say it. Keep your tongue in your head. And I did.

"Signora, I swear to you I'd still be there if my breasts hadn't been so sore. Oh, how they hurt! That's what Minguccio saw. He couldn't make peace with himself about that — everything else — but not that. He came in February to see me, that was the excuse, but he really wanted to ask about that job they'd said they might be able to find him. *La Carogna* let him sit in the kitchen all day. I was there some of the time, but not most of the time, what with the shift back and forth to school and the nursing. That's why he came in to talk to me when I was doing it and saw me sitting there crying and saw my breasts, how they were. And he said, 'We're going home, you and me. I don't care if we starve, you're not going to be maimed.' And he made me pack, and we left that night, and they wouldn't even pay me the 180,000 they owed me or the train ticket. The Colonel finally said, 'Well, just out of the kindness of my heart. Mind you, I don't *owe* you anything. I consider this a month on-trial. Don't forget you've had your room and board too. But just out of the kindness of my heart, I'll give you 70,000 *lire*. Take it or leave it.' In the end we took it."

That was the last time I saw Peppina. She told me she could fight no longer. Minguccio was not sick in his body, but in his mind. He could not stand to go back to Germany alone. Either he found work at home, or she and the children went with him. She had put it off until one of the boys was out of school. He would stay with one of the innumerable sisters-in-law and be apprenticed to a mechanic. Rosa would live with another sister-in-law. The others . . . "Well, they're young," she said. "Maybe they can learn German. Anyway, they'll go to school there. I don't want my children to grow up German, but I guess they will. I have to go."

They arrived in time for the crisis in the German

building industry. Minguccio still works at night in the café, they rent two rooms nearby, but it is Peppina once more, cleaning schools and shopping for women better off than she, who supports them. One thing has gone well for them: no children have been born. Minguccio has been promised work next spring.

When I think of Peppina, I always remember the way she starts her conversations, her shrug and then — "Eh, what can you expect? *Nothing.*"

"That's my house, if you can call it that, and
I'm lucky because I have a window and
nothing in front of it but the hill across the
way. At least we've got air. It's just one room
and there are five of us. It was all right when
the children were little, real little, but
Antonio's five now and he sees things and
hears things he shouldn't. We've applied for
one of the new houses every time we could.
We don't have water, the roof leaks and the
owner won't fix it because we're behind in the
rent. It's 60,000 lire a year ($95), and we just
don't have it this year. My husband worked in
Milan for two years on some kind of
construction, but he got laid off last winter
and there's no work here — that's one thing
you can count on. Now I'm going to have
another baby. And to think they say you
can't get pregnant as long as you're nursing!
I'm nursing two — that's how we make out
— and still. Anyway, we'll ask the Comune
for a house again. I'd be happy with one of
those apartments with two bedrooms, but
it's just an exercise — asking — that is. The
places they're building now are for the people
who lost their houses in the landslide four,
no five years ago. We won't get one."

Ninetta

One June morning I woke up with a peculiar, heavy feeling. It can only be some physical reaction to barometric change, but I accept it now as a warning that everything in the day will go wrong. Outside the sky was blue and cloudless, the air warm. In the courtyard below women, their chores forgotten for the moment, stood gossiping in the shadows near a pig tied to the railing of a first floor balcony. A puppy chased a chicken through a pile of rubble where four small children, naked, were playing. Solina has already put them out for the day, I thought. She had nine and in the summer gave the little ones clothes only on Sunday: her vacation from laundry, she said. What our neighbors called thrift in themselves, they labelled "the slatternly way of a foreigner" in Solina, for she was Slovene, a war bride of twenty years before, who was always referred to, with a slight curl of the lip, as *La Slava*. The garbage cart rattled into the clearing and the collector in his grimy blue smock crawled down from the bicycle seat slowly and a bit stiffly as though it were noon. This was his moment of glory: to announce his presence in the neighborhood, he must blow his whistle. The children and even the women turned to watch him, for his performance — his flamboyant gestures, shrills and tootlings — was considered one of the town's great spectacles. It was all normal enough for a June morning.

I dressed and ate my breakfast to the accompaniment of voices screeching on the stairway in a friendly exchange of complaints, and when all was quiet, I started downstairs, a bit furtively. Maybe if I could postpone involvement with the world — but it was a childish stratagem, destined to fail on the first landing where Ninetta was swirling her mop around with the exaggerated concentration of someone pretending not to lie in wait. She was a lonely woman. For several years her husband had been away, working first in Germany and now in Milan. Her parents were dead, and her only sister had gone north to work in the rice fields, had married and stayed there. Ninetta was the tier gossip and not illogically, the quickest to imagine a slight. Her neat, square body blocked my way without any apparent intention. She turned, giving me a surprised, innocent smile as much as to say, Fancy meeting you here. Definitely she had something on her mind.

Had her life been different her large hazel eyes might have had the wide, ingenuous look of a curious child; instead they were always slightly veiled in calculation. Deep sockets and the heavy arched bones of the eyebrows made them appear darker than they were and somehow at variance with her broad, flat, guileless face. Usually her light brown hair hung in tight curls, but could, when it was clean — always for Christmas, Easter and the *festa* — foam around her head in an angelic halo of curls. Her personality offered the same contradictions. Two characters seemed to live in the same body: one, gentle, kind and retiring; the other, aggressive with a vicious tongue, both in rage and in humor, and so tense that anything she said crackled with her anticipation of a fight. In spite of the vagaries of her disposition, she was known as "a good woman, poor thing," and "poor" not as a financial condition, for everyone was, but "poor" because she had a jealous husband who drank too much and beat her, and a five year old boy, the youngest of her four, with the same large, and in him wondering, hazel eyes, who had been born "without a penis." All over the world defects are mysterious gifts mothers, never fathers, bestow on their children — the result of a defective gene, a shock, an excess or even, we know now, medicines not carefully tested. And it is the mother who bears so much of the daily pain. If, in the normal way, Ninetta bargained for an egg, she could be prepared for twits. If she were involved in some more serious disagreement, she would be emotionally disemboweled, once again, by her opponent's gleeful invective. They had so many weapons to use against her, and all were irresistible to people who expect few victories in life and have never known one too cheap. Ninetta would retreat, but never concede defeat, and so we who shared the stairs with her lived in a state of permanent uncertainty: would we meet a wounded lioness or a purring kitten? Experience had taught us to let her speak first.

"Ah, you're up!" she said, as though surprised, but she smiled: she was in a gentle phase. The insinuation of some failing was an unconscious technique that she had used for her protection until it had become a habit of speech and probably of mind. Still she did not move.

"Now you're here, I wanted to ask you — ah — that is — I wanted to ask if you wanted some tomatoes?" She rushed on without waiting for an answer. "They're the first ones, and, and you like tomatoes," she added with a touch of belligerence.

Soon after I moved in, she had brought me a few figs, then some *rughetta* she picked along the road on her way to the fields, and finally in the fall, when there had been no more produce she could bring, she brought what she cherished most — catastrophes, any, that is, that had happened to someone else. She milked them for comfort. Slowly winter, cold and dark and seemingly endless, imposed a curfew on us. In the mornings, no matter what the weather, muffled figures scurried about doing errands, but early in the afternoon banks of fog swirled in front of our windows, bringing a false, cotton twilight and a silence without echoes. It was easy to believe no one else existed. At first Ninetta had seemed relieved by the isolation, but, as the weeks went on, her problems became the all-invading monsters of hallucinations and to escape them she had come up to talk to me. She knew I could not help her, but perhaps more important to her, I neither condemned her, nor gossiped about her.

"Not now, you understand. Later. I did want to talk to you too — when you have time. No, no, no, not now! I know, not now. Besides you have a flat tire. You'll have to change it." Her smile broadened in something like pleasure. "I saw it when I came in, but don't worry. I'll help you." The cycle had begun: this was the first of the misadventures I had dreaded. Ninetta knew nothing about a car and by help she meant supportive company, but she would not be discouraged. She leaned her mop against the wall, wiped her hands on her apron and then turned to thump purposefully down the stairs.

Fifteen minutes later the tire was changed. I was dirty to the elbows, but forced myself to put the tools away carefully while Ninetta sat on a fruit crate, prim as a duenna, lecturing a group of women and children who had collected to watch me. She had covered the defects of modern tires, their poor resistance to nails and their even poorer wearing qualities and had managed a lightning transition to the elements in aluminum that cause cancer, when suddenly behind me, but still at some distance, a woman's voice shrilled in the sirenlike wail of rage which, like the rattling of a rattlesnake, is the Mediterranean woman's warning of savage attack. As I turned a figure in a blue cotton dress plunged past me with her arms outstretched. The sallow, peaked face of a little boy standing at Ninetta's shoulder screwed up with fear. He stumbled back and then ran as fast as he could up the ramp to the road. His mother veered slightly to grab Ninetta by the hair.

"Whore! Bitch in heat — that's what you are," she screamed, shaking Ninetta until it seemed her neck must snap. "Corrupt my son, will you! Not enough that you lay in wait for my husband!" Ninetta's hands were clawing at the woman's face, her dress, any part of her they could reach. "God's wrath didn't teach you! A boy without his Thing didn't teach you! No, not you! You don't give a damn." She began to kick Ninetta who had fallen backward and was scrambling to untangle herself from the fruit crate. The neighbors dragged the woman off and tried to hold her, though against the strength generated by rage and adrenalin, they could do little more than delay her. Just as she twisted loose, I picked up Ninetta.

She was crying and seemed stunned, but she whirled away from me to attack the woman with kicks and slaps and bites that sent them both to the ground in a tangle of arms and legs. We could hear Ninetta's voice howling over and over again.

"*Sei pazza, pazza, Pazza, PAZZA!*" You're crazy, crazy, Crazy, CRAZY!

Eventually we separated them. We forced Ninetta into the front seat of my car, and I sat with her while the women blocked the door, and she cried. One eye was already pink and swelling. Once she tried, head down, to butt her way past the women, but sank back beside me and sobbed quietly. I asked what the fight was about, who the woman was. They all talked at once. Giulia — for that was the woman's name — was no favorite. She was Ninetta's sister-in-law, they had married brothers, and was so jealous of Ninetta that whenever she could, no matter how thin the excuse, she picked a fight with her. She also wrote anonymous letters to Pietro, Ninetta's husband, accusing her of anything from beating the children to having a lover, jabs perfectly calculated to confirm Pietro's suspicions. He always remembered that there was a small crumb of truth in such letters, but never that the writer is more interested in causing trouble than conveying information. He made Ninetta suffer for every one he ever received.

Suddenly I realized that I knew the reason for Giulia's accusation and I was weighing the evils of betraying what Ninetta had told me must be a secret against the advantages of establishing her innocence, when I heard her, too exasperated to protect anyone, blubbering out the whole story. Without telling Giulia, her husband had borrowed money from Pietro who had told Ninetta to collect it whenever she needed it. She had waited, had accepted her brother-in-law's excuses and delays until recently when she had had no choice. In an effort to be tactful, she had not gone to the house. Rather she had waited for him on the road to ask, yet another time, about the money. Finally the night before he had brought it to her only to have her refuse to open her door. She wanted to avoid trouble. She would not have him in the house and ordered him to leave the money with me. He did, and she collected it as soon as his footsteps could be heard outside on the road.

"I'm no whore," she said through her tears. "As God is my witness, no one comes in my house when I'm alone. You know that, signora. You'd hear anyone, wouldn't you? Tell them, tell them!" She cried, and they started cursing Giulia. Two of them said that if Ninetta would go upstairs they would sit with her and see that she was left in peace.

I went on to have my tire mended, knowing that I could be of more use in the evening when the others were busy with their families. The electricity was off and so there was no air pressure. Later in the day — perhaps — my tire would be returned to me.

Ninetta always lived from one emergency to the next, treating each as a dress rehearsal for disaster. While her physical battle with her sister-in-law was unusual, all scenes were played at the level of high drama and with instinctive precision. She knew her audiences well. She enjoyed an argument; her mind was more flexible than most, her voice, louder. Her insults were quick and panoramic, but her *forte*, readily acknowledged by the other women, was the manipulation of welfare agencies. She wheedled medicines from them, wept and howled and threw her arms around until they gave her blankets and warm overcoats. She has been known to faint with great dignity (and despair) when pleading for *pasta*, though the technique she rather preferred was an hysterical fit of crying. It came more easily to her, she said. Still she would admit that in some situations a prolonged faint drew enough attention. She attacked every other facet of her existence with the same immediate and absolute concentration and was as a result an extremely adroit, fast worker in the fields, an efficient housekeeper, a good if unpredictable mother and the general terror of the neighborhood. This informal *modus vivendi* of bully life first lest it bully you excluded all need for thought: it was enough to react.

For Ninetta it worked well until little Giuseppe was born "without a penis." (I continue to put the phrase in quotation marks because it was hers and because Giuseppe is the only child who never wandered around wearing a cotton undershirt and nothing else. Ninetta would have killed the child rather than let anyone see him, so I have no idea how accurate the description was medically, but five operations performed in the first seven years of his life tend to confirm it.)

Now she had time to brood and reason. Suddenly arguments and exchanges of insults which had been her tournament weapons were sharpened for blood sport, and if her scenes with the welfare representatives were just as florid, they were somehow less effective: they were no longer part of a game she could afford to lose. Now when she really needed help, she had lost her touch. No one was willing or able, she never knew which. She began to see demons. She imagined strange, elaborate schemes against her. She brooded in a way no one had expected, though it was not surprising, for she did it as she did everything else — with relentless zeal.

Her fights with her husband Pietro had always been one of the squalid realities of modern tissue-paper housing that we all accepted. He was a big, powerful man with a spongy face and curly, reddish hair, who as an on-the-stair acquaintance was almost timid, certainly not violent. He was soft-spoken, always insisted on carrying my packages, even ridiculously light ones, and had an almost obsequious way of pressing himself back against the plaster to let me pass as though he expected it to fold around him and so remove his contaminating presence. Sometimes on market days he followed Ninetta from stall to stall with the same gentle thoughtfulness. Wine only exaggerated his courtesies to me and, I learned, his brutality to his wife. After months of listening to their quarrels I came to several disconcerting conclusions: that *both* were jealous, *both* given to imagining flirtations and outright infidelities where they knew none existed and that *both* enjoyed the fights as a more prosperous city couple might a meal out or a cinema — these were their twice-weekly amusements. His mother, who lived with them and who, depending on the weather, spent her days at the bedroom window or on the balcony, spying on all that happened below, goaded first Ninetta, whom she despised, then Pietro with reports of the other's misconduct as witnessed by her. She, of course, had a front row seat for the inevitable match and could be heard urging her son on, even congratulating him for a particularly well-aimed blow at Ninetta.

The second summer after Giuseppe was born, with the coming of warm weather, open windows and late

evenings sitting on our balconies, we in the neighborhood could hardly avoid realizing that Ninetta and Pietro's fights had changed. There was no question of
eavesdropping: we had no choice. Along with the squalls
of teething babies and radios, their voices joined us at
dinner, kept us company through the dishes, billowed up
around us like clouds of poisonous gas as we drank coffee and pursued us to bed where, finally, in spite of
them, we fell asleep nervous and exhausted. More often
than not we would awaken sometime later to heavy thuds,
punctuated by Ninetta's screams of agony — or perhaps rage, it was hard to tell. No one would approach
their door; we had heard too many benighted intruders
driven away by their chorus of threats and curses.

We were so accustomed to the fights that, at first,
when the tone changed, none of us bothered to listen. My
impression is still that I never did, that the words seeped
into my brain by osmosis. Now it was Ninetta who talked.
Pietro and his mother provided a grumbling continuo of
si's, *no*'s and *ma*'s, which, if they became too insistent,
Ninetta cut off with a sharp, "*Basta!* Shut up, both of
you. *Basta*, I say!" And her voice would grind on at a
lower pitch which carried surprisingly well to all of us
sitting in the dark.

The pivotal words that we heard repeated night
after night were "work" and "insurance," "here, no,"
"there, yes," but if the beginning and the middle of the
scenes were totally controlled by Ninetta, the finale remained Pietro's. One extra word, half a glass more of
wine and his fury would explode into the bellows and
sickening soft thuds that we knew meant the end was
near. And then instead of silence and muffled sniffling,
Ninetta's voice suddenly very quiet would say,

66

"*Basta,* Pietro. It's useless to yell that way. We've got to decide." She already had.

Pietro was satisfied with his usual cycle of work. He was very strong, never missed a day, and never caused trouble. As a result he was seldom unemployed. The outside contractors who usually won the bids for the construction of public buildings were glad to pay a dependable man his legal salary and insurance contributions. Because of the extreme cold the men were laid off from late fall to early spring and the site closed down, but Pietro never worried. He simply found work in town and asked for a few hundred *lire* a day more than usual in lieu of insurance. Pietro was happy. He had a bit extra *and* for as long as the period of "unemployed" grace lasted his medical insurance as well. The employer had a good workman and could savor that sweetest of all pleasures to a Southerner, the evasion of another payment to his government. Pietro took the risks. The employer could always claim he had only hired him for two or three days' work.

When Giuseppe was born, Ninetta realized that if they were ever to put him right, they could do without everything except the health insurance which would see to his hospitalization, his medicines, his operations and perhaps in time even a pension. And so she had decided: Pietro must go to Germany with a work contract, which, under an agreement between the two governments, meant automatic payment of Italian insurances and a high salary. Pietro insisted there was no reason for him to go: he was never without work, they ate well and were together. Only weaklings need run away to find work: he was no weakling. On and on it would go until finally we would hear one terrible roar from Pietro, followed im-

67

mediately by a heavy crash and sometimes a splintering of wood and then silence, almost more harrowing than the scene that had preceded it, announced the end of hostilities for the night.

Within the month the arguments had changed again, not in decibels or violence, but in subject, as though the basic issue had been decided. Pietro's jeers and roars were all about the work contract. "Sure, sure, just like that I can get one! With half Lucania trying! *Ma che cazzo vuoi!* What do you know about it? Nothing! NOTHING!" or sometimes, "*You* go out and whore for it, if you're so sure, but if you do, don't show your ass back here."

Ninetta never talked about their fights. Undoubtedly she knew she did not have to, nor did she discuss her plans. Obviously Pietro felt entirely safe and he should have. Hundreds of thousands of men went to Germany clandestinely, the "wet-backs" of the Mediterranean, in search of employment no matter how temporary, willing to work at cut rates and without insurance. Other thousands scrounged for the few hundred official contracts offered. If a man could convince a friendly clerk in the town hall to issue a certificate guaranteeing the holder to be a master electrician, carpenter, plumber or a wizard at some other skill that looked promising, then he could start soliciting recommendations. It is a time-honored system in which every Southerner believes. No matter what his qualifications, real or certified, he knows there is no hope without recommendations. If a friend of the sister-in-law of his wife's second cousin married a Deputy's chauffeur, then he can maneuver for a testimonial that will carry some weight, but if he has no such close tie, he must count on numbers to make up for quality. In this treasure hunt almost any man who wears a white shirt and black shoes and almost any woman in kid pumps who carries a leather purse is a possible asset. They can, at least, write, and they might even have connections. It is a slow, degrading process of wheedling, promising, threatening and cringing and more often than not absolutely futile. Certainly Pietro had no intention of wasting his time. Ninetta had no acquaintanceship among the *"notabili"* except the landowners for whom she had worked, and they were neither apt to help nor would they be listened to if they did.

Indeed, Pietro felt entirely safe.

Weeks later, when the impasse had become a permanent element of their fights and we thought nothing more, a list was posted in the government employment office naming twelve qualified pipe fitters from Puglia and Lucania who had been accepted as helpers with official work contracts, insurance and all legal benefits by a German chemical complex. Pietro, who could build concrete forms, but had never touched a pipe, was one of them. They were given ten days in which to order their affairs, as though they had any, and obtain their identity cards and insurance papers.

Pietro was seized by a cataleptic melancholy. He spent his days sitting on his balcony, looking at nothing; his nights, wandering back and forth along the road, sidestepping into the deep shadows at the sound of voices. In the days before he left there were no more scenes. He spoke to no one outside his own house and seldom even then to Ninetta who, if he stayed out in the dark too long, would go down and urge him to come to bed. Once, as they came back together, I heard him ask,

"How did you do it?"

"Doesn't make any difference now how I did it. The important thing is that it's done. You have the job. And I didn't whore for it either."

I believe her, but I know nothing more than that about how she arranged it. She only smiled when asked and slipped her eyes off sideways as though they would give her away. It is her secret and she has kept it, even from Pietro, though it is not hard to guess that she found a way to blackmail the right person.

Finally one bleak, gray September morning, just after dawn, Pietro left with six or seven others who were determined to try illegally. The bus for the station twenty miles below in the valley was late, but the men seemed too dazed to notice. Like so many pale stiff cadavers awaiting their coffins, they lined up facing the road and just stood there. Their wives with shawls pulled over their heads and around their shoulders against the first cold were nervous. Babies slept in their arms, others clung sleepily to their skirts and whined for food, but their mothers ignored them. They were not travelers. They were anxious. Would the men miss their connection? Would the food packed in the pathetic assortment of bundles and cardboard suitcases at their feet, would it be enough? One or two wept quietly. An older woman hissed a warning to her son about loose women, which he pretended not to hear. His wife blushed, but said nothing. Ninetta was silent too, but as she watched Pietro her huge eyes filled with tears which did not quite escape to run down her cheeks. His attention was held by something invisible just beyond the tip of his scuffed boots. At last the bus swung around the curve with the special trumpeting of the three-note horn common to Italian country buses of the period. The women had waited too long to have time for a satisfying wail. Before they could screw up their faces, their husbands had planted that dry impersonal peck on each cheek which is the acceptable public kiss, had fumbled and kicked their bundles to the baggage hatch, lifted them up and then disappeared into the bus, which with another trumpet snorted off, leaving the women and children to gasp in the oily black cloud of its exhaust. The men were gone.

"He's finally convinced it's right," Ninetta said in a low, tired voice as we walked back from the bus stop. "Finally! All he said before he left was 'I warn you if you put horns on me I'll come back and kill you. Do you understand? I'll kill you.' As if I'd have time with all I've got to do — let's forget the urge. But he says that sort of thing when he goes to work right here in town, so he didn't have much on his mind when he left. He's convinced all right. Finally."

Ninetta's life was much as it had been. She had plenty of work cutting and hauling firewood. She was careful to pick men with whom she had worked before, men who would leave her alone and paid her in wood, a fixed percentage of the day's take. Later when winter brought an end to all of life in the fields, she looked for chores in town. She, like Pietro, was strong and seldom unemployed simply because she would do anything — wrestle barrels, load sacks, chop stove lengths, clean stalls, wash laundry — she was not finicky if she was well and promptly paid.

There was one radical change. The day after Pietro left she moved her mother-in-law out, mattress, bedsprings, bundles of clothes, favorite copper pots, lighted Madonna and all, to the apartment of another son and daughter-in-law, the venomous Giulia. I was driving

71

home for lunch when I came up behind Ninetta in the middle of the road, carrying the bedsprings, feet up, on her head. With each step they dipped precariously, hesitated and then swooped up and forward in a slow tidal movement. Ninetta must have had more control over this undulating monster than was apparent, for she used only one hand to brace it as she swung around to talk to me. It almost escaped to twirl like a helicopter propeller, but she caught it. Her face lit up with a mischievous smile.

"Eh," she said with that odd jerk of the chin out and upward which means, Watch me, I'll show them. "This is the day! From now on, like it or not like it, she can tell *them* what to do. This is one penance I don't have to make!" As she turned to go on, she laughed out loud with the kind of childish pleasure that could disintegrate into giggles. "Let her try the *dolce vita* over there!" And off she went dipping and swaying.

That winter she took Giuseppe to Bari for the first operation. She said nothing about it to anyone, not even, it turned out, to her mother-in-law who had been reinstated — the flow of mattress, bedsprings, bundles, copper pots and lighted Madonna having been reversed for the first of many times — to look after the other children. Giuseppe was to have "tests."

One day when Ninetta had been gone almost two weeks I was given a message which, though addressed to me, was for Ninetta's mother-in-law. I could imagine the keeper of the Bar Italia, who was also the custodian of the public telephone, scribbling it with his right hand, while with his left he pulled down the lever on the coffee machine or dragged a grimy rag over the counter. I had watched him do it dozens of times and had listened to him shout, "What's that? Say it again," as the paper jumped and skipped on its own, leaving squiggles stranded inches below the word they might belong to. The result was always something of a Chinese puzzle, but it was not his fault. The telephone, which had to be kept on the back counter out of reach of the longest arm, had accumulated around it a nest of torn telephone books, sticky cups and spoons, bottle caps and drying pastries. Writing was almost impossible, but then anyone who called in a message had to be a patient optimist and a gambler, if not an outright fool. Our telephone service had an erratic, one-way quality. Depending on the winds and atmospheric pressures of all the points through which the line passed, we could either hear clearly and not be heard at all, or we could be heard, but were ourselves rationed to sweeping sighs, crackles and intriguing snatches of other people's conversations — "All right, you want two tons of foam rubber at 800 *lire*," or "Enrico thought it was heart trouble, but the specialist says it's only corns" — which faded back to splutters and burps, when I, for one, would have renounced all contact with my "party" to hear more.

Under these conditions any message had to be accepted as ninety percent clairvoyance: Ninetta's was no exception. If she nourished an instinctive distrust of mechanical contraptions, like most people who use them seldom, she had even less faith in the good offices of the human being, thus the message addressed to me. With exquisite social precision she had decided that what would reach me immediately would never be delivered to her mother-in-law, though in fairness, the difference in attitude depended as much on greed for the one hundred *lire* tip I gave the bar-owner's little boy as it did on class and respect. My supposed social standing did not rate any clarification of the text. It seemed to say: Everyone pretty for next week, send taxes to Bari Hospital at 12 noon today 8o." It sounded like a coded invasion plan, but after a certain amount of anagrammatic manipulation read: All well, cannot return until next week. Send taxi to Bari hospital at noon a week from today.

I took it to Ninetta's mother-in-law and because she was illiterate, read it to her, but she hardly bothered to listen. She had not been worried, she said. She knew Ninetta would come home when she got tired of gallivanting.

"Just like her to do it in style," she grumbled. "A car when the bus'd do as well. I'll send someone, but it's a waste of money. Just like her — always been that way. Plain wasteful. If Pietro was here, he'd tell her . . ."

"She earned the money, so you'll have to let her decide how to use it," was all I said and left her to churn out her complaints to the children who paid no attention, so accustomed were they to the sound of that voice.

No one was surprised at the length of time the "tests" had taken, which proves Ninetta's theory of human indifference and does something to confirm a suspicion of mine that since daily life in such a village is totally egocentric, if someone left or for whatever reason — even no more than a prolonged illness that kept him in bed — disappeared, he ceased to exist for his own neighbors. They might reminisce about him, a dim figure of the past, but only when they met him again — in the market, or along the road, or on the stairs — was he alive, able to get in their way, amuse them, cheat them or help them. Ninetta was gone. She had no reality. Her arrival would be a rebirth. In Italian schools cause and effect reasoning is treated with about the same enthusiasm as the theory of human evolution, but still it seemed odd to me that no one put the extended stay and the hired car together to reach the conclusion that Giuseppe had been in the hospital for an operation and was not yet strong enough to make the trip back on the bus. I was asking them to reanimate her, to think about *her* and of course they would not. Instead they gnawed on the extravagance of the hired car with cannibalistic malice.

It was already dark when they arrived, and no one saw them. In winter we turn our backs to the road and huddle blindly over fires, as though, by warming our hands and feet, we can melt the icy pessimism of our tedious minds. I heard Ninetta come up the stairs slowly, heavily as though she were carrying Giuseppe, and open the door. Then her mother-in-law's voice chattered like an enraged monkey's, and I knew she had begun her catalogue of recriminations. Ninetta never raised her voice; in fact I doubt she said anything. Less than half an hour later the bedsprings squawked in their usual grating way, followed by two deep exhausted sighs, and all was silent for the night.

The next afternoon, when Giuseppe was napping, Ninetta came to see me. Nineteen days and nineteen nights sitting on a chair by his bed, nursing him as an Italian mother is expected to do, worrying over him as any mother would, had taken fifteen or twenty pounds off her square frame. Around her eyes dark circles that extended up into her eyebrows and out onto her cheeks, might almost have been bruises. She was tired, tired, tired, she said, and her voice sounded it. For the first time I saw her sit with her hands still, hooked one over the other in her lap. She had done the best she could there alone. It was better, wasn't it, to avoid a second trip? After the tests the doctor had told her he could operate. She would have to take the responsibility. He had been brusque. Her only chance to talk to him was in the corridor as he sailed from one ward to the next with a convoy of young men — doctors and technicians, she thought — whose primary function was to ward off the relatives of patients.

"The boss specialist was no hundred *lire* doctor like what we get here. You couldn't offer him homemade *salame* and fresh eggs to get his attention," she said. "But he wouldn't help me. He hardly looked at me when he talked, like maybe I was diseased or a whore or something. And all he'd say was 'I am a doctor. It is my job to operate, not to comfort wailing mothers and grandmothers.' He was never like that with Giuseppe though. He was patient with him and gentle. He gave me two days to decide because either way Giuseppe had to have some kind of shots they were giving him. The last morning I waited until he'd finished on our floor and then I stood in the middle of the corridor with my hands on my hips and said, 'This time you've got to listen to me.' A nun tried to drag me out of his way, but he said, 'No, Sister, leave her.' So I said I'd do it if he'd explain to me, tell me what they were going to do and you know what he said? He said, I swear he did — 'It's too complicated for you to understand.' That's what he said. They're all God Almighty, those doctors. But he did say I'd made the right decision, if I wanted the child to be right. He told me to sign the papers in the office, so that next morning he could operate, and then he pushed by me just like I wasn't there.

"I was so tired. When they took Giuseppe out for the tests every morning I used to curl up on his bed and

76

fall asleep, but if a nun caught you, you were in for trouble. There was a woman with a baby in the bed right next to us — he died, *pover'anima*, two days ago — she used to poke me if she heard anyone coming. We took turns at night. I'd sleep sitting in the chair with my head on my arms on the bed, and she'd watch out that Giuseppe didn't need me and I did the same for her, but that's not really sleep. After a few days I ran out of food. There was a place where I could buy bread, but they were crooks, the people who ran it. Everything was double priced. I was pretty hungry by the time they operated on Giuseppe, but then for a few days I could eat what they brought him from the cart. He didn't want it.

"That doctor's a funny man. After they brought Giuseppe back, he sent a doctor every hour or two to look at him, see that he was all right. He wouldn't let the nurses touch him either. He changed the bandages and fiddled with the tubes himself, or one of the others did. He told me he'd rather teach *me* to do it than to try to teach a nun. At least once I learned, I'd do it right, he said. He'd been so nice; then all of a sudden a week ago, one morning he started swearing at me in front of all those women because Giuseppe's bed was dirty. You won't believe it, but I couldn't say anything — not a thing. It was the others who told him no one had given me any sheets — or them either, for that matter. Then we had the end of the world. That was a *real* scene! It all came out, how we had no water to mop off the kids and how the nuns wouldn't let us get near the tubs they had filled. The water only ran a couple of hours a day. Well, after that didn't we have a fancy ward with clean sheets and bottles of bath water and water to drink every morning! And every day the nun would say to us, 'Now you be

77

sure and tell the Professor what good care we're taking of you.'

"Yesterday before we left he told me what to do and to come back in three months, so he can see Giuseppe. Then next fall, or maybe even before, he'll operate again. He said, 'You see, I told you everything would be all right.' And I never opened my mouth, but, signora, he didn't say any such thing. I promised him an Easter cake with *ricotta* and he even smiled. So I'll go back. I guess I'll go back as many times as I have to, but it'll never be as bad again. I know what to expect now — and next time I'll take more food too." She sighed as though she would like to close her eyes and go to sleep, and then suddenly she laughed. "There, I got that out of my system. Now I'll go move the old hag," and she jerked her thumb down toward the floor. "Back down the road she goes for some more *dolce vita.*" In that instant she looked almost like herself.

After her trip to Bari she talked less perhaps, but she did not brood and she could still be tempted by an especially titillating bit of gossip. One clear Sunday morning after Mass four women came to enjoy the warmth of her balcony before going home to cook lunch, and I heard her tell her story of the operation with a few artistic exaggerations and heroic renditions of her conversations with the specialist. I could imagine the drama of the gestures which accompanied them. From their murmurs I knew the women were impressed. Ninetta is an adept, natural raconteur and too shrewd to blunt her effect or risk boring her audience with constant repetition. I think she gave one or two performances and then let the story travel on its own. Two things are certain: she was treated with new respect and she was the undisputed authority to be consulted by anyone who had to take a sick child to Bari.

She slipped back into her normal life except that now Giuseppe went where she did. Each morning she would see that the other children were up and getting ready to go to school before she left for whatever work she had found. Giuseppe was already fed and dressed, upholstered really, in every wool sweater he had, two pairs of trousers, rubber boots and over it all a patched overcoat that came almost to his boot tops and kept his arms immobilized away from his body at a twenty minutes of five position. On his head was a leather helmet, too large for him and with a visor that had been well chewed by a dog. When Ninetta snapped the strap under his chin, fixing the ear flaps, which she never failed to do before they went outside, his thin little face with the eyes bigger than ever before almost disappeared. He looked like a sad miniature scarecrow. When he got tired, and he still tired easily, he would sleep in the cab of a truck or propped up on a chair in the post office or in the back of the tobacco shop. Ninetta was taking no chances. He could be hurt playing with other children, or worse, he could be teased with that infallible savagery the young have for the weaknesses of their companions.

As long as winter lasted her delaying tactic worked well enough and Giuseppe grew stronger, more able to fend for himself, but with summer the time had come, as it had to, when he wanted to be freer, out of doors and not tied to her heels. So began what was to be the drama of each day. At least once, often two or three times if Ninetta were not working, Giuseppe would come up the stairs sobbing in a half howl, half cry that, like a spasm, seemed to invade every muscle of his body. When he

79

arrived at their landing, he would rest his head on the door and start pounding with his fists and screaming.

"Ma! Ma! Open up, Ma!" and then more sobs until finally Ninetta would open the door, scoop him up and rock him in her arms. I have watched it dozens and dozens of times. He had been excluded from a game and sent to play with the girls, or they had dared him to "*fare pipi*" in front of them, or they had teased him about his diapers. Seldom had he been hurt, unless he had fallen the way all children do. While his fright and rage and hurt feelings were tragic and sounded even more so than they were, what always sent a shiver down my spine was Ninetta's reaction. Once she was sure he was unhurt, she charged down the stairs, screeching as I imagine a banshee would.

"*Mo ta'ccide eeyeee! Mo ta'ccide eeyeee!*" And it was easy to believe she would kill. Several times she beat children very badly before she could be stopped: one of them had had nothing to do with the incident. At the sound of her voice the children learned to dash for cover, and mothers rushed to their courtyard windows to make sure one of their own was not about to be killed. Often adults in the courtyard had grabbed the culprit and boxed his ears before Ninetta came plunging out to do battle, her face congested and twisted in uncontrollable hatred. They reasoned with her, calmed her until finally, still churning with rage, but resigned, she would go back upstairs to Giuseppe. He forgot almost as soon as he stopped crying, but for Ninetta it was not so easy. While he sat nibbling at a hunk of bread with a sliver of pepper mashed on it, she questioned him about who had said what, had anyone hit him and had they thrown things at him. For the rest of the day she goaded herself with the silent repetition of these cruelties, refurbishing old feuds and picking the seeds of new ones, until she collapsed in a self-induced state of nervous exhaustion, a pattern which would be revived with the morning and the first crisis of that day.

There was no escape for her and slowly her tension had its effect on the children. The eldest girl, a pretty child with blond curly hair and light green eyes, cried at the first sign of trouble. If she had done anything wrong, or if not actually wrong, that irritated her mother, she flew into a tantrum so uncontrolled that it was almost a fit. Ninetta, whose education (she reads and writes) had not included psychology, could not bear the noise and was frightened by the rigid muscles. Her remedy was to lock the child out in the hall, calculating that she would want to get back in and would understand that to do so she must stop yowling. The theory might have been right for another child, but in practice it simply added another piercing sound to our already cacophonous hallway. Ninetta did not mean to be unkind. She thought the child, who was nervous anyway, was anxious over the fifth grade, the last and most important in the elementary school, which ends in a state examination. A great many children had to repeat the fifth, but the fault was not entirely theirs: the teachers, out of laziness, or perhaps inattention, or a desire to please (or at least not displease), did not fail them in the earlier grades or warn them that their work was substandard. The examination did the winnowing, so many children at the prospect of disapproval and shame did become very tense. This child was not one of them; school was the only peaceful place in her life. A boy, a year younger, tried to avoid the scenes by never being at home, which with his appetite was hard. Soon he was caught stealing cheese in the market, then he broke into an abandoned house and Ninetta was beside herself. If she lectured him or beat him, he was docile, waiting until she had finished and then, after getting some bread from the cupboard, he would go out to disappear until late at night. The younger girl did not worry Ninetta as much. She was only five or six and could not really escape her mother's will, but she was trying. When no one was watching, she was mean to Giuseppe. She never actually hurt him, but delighted in petty tortures, twisting his arm or pulling his hair or pinching his leg until he screamed, always, of course, when their mother was busy elsewhere. She wanted and demanded attention that Ninetta seldom had time enough to supply.

She worried about all of them and if she did not know exactly *what* was wrong, she knew something was. She came up to talk to me about them; she undoubtedly talked to others too. Finally by trial and error she worked out a schedule that allayed the worst of the symptoms and brought a relative, if temporary peace. When she worked all day in the fields, the younger girl went with her. The girl who had tantrums looked after Giuseppe, did battle for him when necessary, and curiously that was less and less often. The older boy was asked to do one thing: present himself at home for supper every evening. Ninetta came back and cooked a meal (sometimes nothing more than a *pasticcio* of stale bread, but hot at least) just as though it were Sunday. They no longer ate in waves as they arrived or the urge took them, but together, sitting down.

The summer passed. Pietro came home for three weeks and the scenes started again, following the original pattern of jealousies and imagined infidelities. Grandmother, paraphernalia and family gods, had been moved back temporarily to root from the sidelines and in general cause as much trouble as she could. There were no fights about work. Pietro was returning and quite proudly, it seemed. When he left, grandmother was not moved out, and I wondered what new project Ninetta might be planning. In three weeks she was gone, leaving the children who were in school to the care of their complaining, but able-bodied grandmother. Giuseppe went with her, where, no one knew.

When she finally came back at Christmas, she told us she had gone to Germany, not however with Pietro. German medicine has earned an almost mythical reputation in Southern Italy, and Ninetta had decided Giuseppe should be seen by a German specialist, who would confirm the Bari diagnosis, or if not, would carry out the proper treatment. She did not want any "insurance doctor," so Pietro was of no use to her. After only she knows how many nights of worry and plans, she figured out that her best chance would be through a convent. Nuns could give her work, they would let Giuseppe stay with her and might help her find the right doctor. She could not apply for a passport for herself or for Giuseppe without written consent from Pietro. Identity cards were dubious travel documents and not yet fully accepted within Common Market countries. That is what she had and what she used for her first trip beyond Naples. Somehow she crossed four frontiers going and four returning. Once, at least, a man in her compartment agreed to say he was her husband and she had not had time to get a passport. One night and perhaps more she spent in a freight car. In Milan the station police stopped her for vagrancy and soliciting, but she was able to show her ticket to Basel, her money and her light luggage and explain that she had been trying to ask which track she should go to for her train. They released her. She walked across at least one border in the dark. She seems to have had no fear of what might have happened if she were caught.

"Eh, at the worst, the very worst, they'd send me home, and that would mean I'd forgotten how to talk. I knew I could get out of anything — I could convince them."

It did not occur to her that she might not reach Germany. Who would keep a mother from caring for her child? German was a shock to her. She had expected a language more like an unfamiliar Italian dialect. Once she realized how incomprehensible it was, she polled her traveling companions for the names of towns where someone spoke Italian. They seemed to agree on one place whose name she has never been able to pronounce well enough for me to find it on a map, but where she spent just over two months. Indeed, she found a convent, convinced the nuns to let her work in the kitchen for her room and board and begged them to help her find the right doctor for Giuseppe. Apparently one nun spoke some Italian: all were uniformly kind to her. She talked with wonder of their charity to anyone who came to their door — of the clothes and food and beds they gave people, of their advice and their comfort. I suspect they were not so unusual, just that they seemed so to Ninetta, for she had stumbled onto that most unlikely of all things to her — a Protestant order of nuns.

She came back because the German doctor confirmed the Bari diagnosis and encouraged her to continue with the operations. Somehow she deceived another four sets of frontier guards, or evaded them, to arrive home, tired but contented. What to a more sophisticated traveler sounds a foolhardy trip, one which logically should have ended at the first border, and if it did not, could be expected to yield little, was instead a total success to Ninetta. For a woman as inexperienced as she, it was a display of bravura hard to equal. It also reassured her about Giuseppe's operations, which continued at regular intervals in Bari.

Pietro returned for Easter to announce that he had no intention of staying in Germany and had, in fact, found work in Milan for the next year *with* insurance, yes, but with no contract. The holiday was a lively one for the neighborhood what with recriminations for Ninetta's "holiday," as he insisted upon calling it, in Germany, and his "going off on an adventure" as Ninetta dubbed his job without security. Mother-in-law, who had been moved back once more with all her chattels, did her utmost to encourage ill-feeling, and again our evenings ended with screams and sickening thuds. It was a relief to everyone when Pietro left, and his mother could be transferred down the road.

And so things seesawed until that June morning when Ninetta "helped" me change my flat tire and in the end fought with her sister-in-law Giulia. She had asked to see me that evening, but she did not come and I had every reason to know why.

At twilight that night the breeze did not rise to cool us. The air was dusty and the miasma of bubbling asphalt, exhaust, scorched chaff, cooking, and becalmed drains choked us. There was no choice: we fled to our balconies until like an audience in some bizarre long, narrow theater, we filled three tiers of boxes on either side of the road and waited for the lights to be dimmed. There was a murmur of voices, but for the most part people were content to sit, fanning themselves. Suddenly across the way and off to my left a woman's voice began to shriek and gabble in dialect. She was so strident, so frenzied that it was hard to understand anything except the obvious obscenities. When she stopped, there was total silence, not the negative lack of sound, but positive, almost tangible silence. Still nothing. She started again.

"Whore, daughter of a whore, mother of whores — that's what you are. That's what you all are! I always said it, and I'll say it again. Whore! Whore! Whore! So now Pietro's gone and it makes you itch, doesn't it? You'll be off traveling again soon! Where to this time, Whore, WHORE?"

"Eyeee, I'd need you for a teacher, you filthy bitch," came an answering screech in almost exactly the same tone, but the voice was fuller and right under my balcony: Ninetta. "To cheat and lie and steal is an art with you! Don't worry, we all know, and someday . . ." She left that to hang in the silence.

"Someday what?"

No answer.

"Some day what?"

"The police will come," Ninetta screamed. "And I'll be glad! Glad! Ehh, too many years gone by? You think you're safe! They can't get you now — can they? You'll see. We all know what you stole, how you sold it. Don't think we don't remember! Remember that certain Antonio? Filth! FILTH is what you are!" From her voice I could tell Ninetta was mad enough to lean out over her railing to yell down the road, but even raving as she was she had won an advantage. Giulia was following her, not leading.

"What do you think you're talking about . . ."

To translate all that was yowled back and forth by those women in the next two hours, and it lasted two full hours, would be to replace horror with the banality of obscene words. It was not just another squalid fight. The rawness of their emotions, their brutality and the tension it generated may be the classic elements of tragedy, but nowhere else could it have been played at such an extreme pitch, no where else would the bystanders have been so lacerated by words which did not concern them. Like *Medea*, it was a totally Mediterranean tragedy, one which could not have taken place, would not have been convincing set in, say, the Norwegian fjords. This was no game — to either of them. Each barrage was leaden with the hurt feelings of the past, the loneliness and the desperation that had found no response. They were not carping. They were finally voicing all the distrust and loathing that had cowered in the foliage of slights and barbs.

"You're not even Christian. When my mother died, you never so much as offered to take the children for an hour."

"Eh, so you're Christian after what you've done to Pietro's mother?"

"We could have starved to death with never so much as an up your ass from you."

"You're so high and mighty, you want to treat the rest of us — even your own family — like goat crap in the road."

Then suddenly there would be silence. We, sitting in the dark, said nothing. We were quieter than quiet. No feet shuffled, no chairs scraped. I never lighted a cigarette: it seemed an intrusion. We were immobile, fighting an inner grinding, almost hysterical tightness that wanted to explode. There was no pattern about the silences or the breaking of them, and no implication of victory. Giulia might have the last word and ten minutes later start on an entirely different tack, as Ninetta could have, but they screamed with equal venom until it seemed their larynxes, their veins, their very heads should rupture, splattering their blood and their lives out on the road in front of us. Once Giulia's mother-in-law dragged her away from the balcony with a great clattering of glass and banging of door frames, but in seconds she was back, roaring out into the dark.

"You say you're not foul. YOU SAY IT! YOU SAY IT! But God knows better. Look at His punishment. Look at Giuseppe! Why was he born without his Thing? Tell me that, *if you're so pure!*"

It all might have ended sooner if Giulia had not resorted to Giuseppe each time her mind went blank and left her with nothing except her black rage. And each time Ninetta charged out to slay the Gorgon. Then, unexpectedly, at the end of one tirade, she stopped, coughed and said in a loud but normal voice,

"*Signore, Signori, andate a letto. Lo spettacolo è finito!*" "Ladies, gentlemen, go to bed. The show is over!" We heard her close the doors to her balcony, and soon after, a light was turned on which sent one lone shaft, like a spotlight, cutting out into the dark. Giulia tried to flush her out again with screeched obscenities, but Ninetta did not appear. If anyone can be said to win such a fight, Ninetta did with the dignity of her retreat.

Slowly with heavy exhausted movements, people got up, moved chairs around, closed shutters and from the noisy dripping sound a few even watered their dusty potted flowers. We went to bed, I, to sleep fitfully, perhaps because of the heat, or perhaps because of the soft lugubrious keening that droned through the night, seemed to surround my bed and echo about the room. Finally toward dawn Ninetta fell asleep too.

For the next ten days she kept very much to herself, leaving early to work, coming home at night to close herself in her house. The neighbors did not try to waylay her, nor did they waste much time discussing the macabre scene, but many of them made simple gestures, which were intended to be anonymous, though the children always seemed to know and undoubtedly told Ninetta. Two eggs would appear in front of the door on a nest of leaves, or a few of the first figs or a bunch of grapes. The children in the courtyard were gentler with Giuseppe, and several of the mothers were so assiduous in offering him snacks that it amounted to forced feeding. He went around with a perpetual smile on his face and soon began to waddle slightly, as though the new weight of his tummy had trifled with his center of gravity.

Ninetta had squabbled with everyone. No incident or comment could pass without a gibe from her. She was an uncomfortable person to have watching the slips and slights and oversights of life, yet she was not malevolent, and they all knew it, as they knew that she was not immoral. If Giulia had accused her of only one constant lover, they would have re-examined Ninetta's every movement and have discovered that they remembered unexplained footsteps on the stairs and those nights she said she was going to see a friend across the road, and-and- and-until the game was not Is there a lover? but What is his name? Giulia's enthusiastic descriptions of wantonness at home, on the road, in Bari, in Germany did not bring the reaction she expected, for Ninetta was automatically exonerated and she, Giulia, was suspect. Such a catalogue, it was said, implied experience. So it was Giulia who suffered the shame of isolation in a house with the shutters closed and the door firmly locked.

Finally one afternoon a week or so after the fight it rained, breaking the heat. At dusk a high wind came up rattling the windows, sucking doors to with a crash. Just above my head on the roof the wind baffle of my stove flue twirled and clattered so furiously that I did not hear the knock at my door until, in a sudden vacuum, the pounding sounded like thunder. When I opened it, Ninetta was standing there, rather dejectedly, with a plate of figs in her hand.

"I brought you these. We've got so many they're going to make us sick," and she stopped, shook her head and laughed. "That's a fine way to give you something, isn't it? But it's the truth and — well, you know what I mean." She closed the door and sat down on a chair near it. "Besides, remember I said I wanted to talk to you — it seems a long time ago now — that day you had the flat tire and — and — I . . . ?" but she never finished. Tears rolled down her cheeks, large, lazy, honest tears.

I took the plate from her and went to the kitchen to make us some coffee. It was one thing she loved and seldom had. Before the pot started its hissing and snorting I could hear her sobbing, very quietly, in the next room. When I returned with our cups, she was scrubbing at her face with a rather dirty handkerchief and her eyes were very red. She did not say much, but sat, looking at her hands in her lap and shaking her head very slowly. In all the years I knew her it was the only time I ever felt she was not ready for battle, that no challenge or insult could call up enough energy for a fight. But she was not defeated; she made that very clear.

"Signora, I've just come to tell you I'm through, I won't take anymore, no matter what Pietro says or anyone else. I won't take anymore." Tears rolled down her cheeks again, but she paid no attention. "I've worked and struggled — and not just for myself — for Giuseppe and the others in this God-forsaken place, and I'll work and struggle some more — somewhere — but not here. They call themselves 'Christians,' but I say they're worse than animals for what they've done to me." She held up her hand to keep me from saying anything. "Yes, I know. Not *all* of them. Not that they'd help me, but they wouldn't hurt me. No, not all of them. That's the worst part — it's my relatives. What have I ever done to them? What? What? Can you tell me? Oh, I know. I get work when they can't. Pietro gets work when they can't — and yes, I know too that I've got a tongue, but not 'til you cross me — really — at least most of the time." She tried to smile, but her mouth only managed a slight twitch.

"I've had plenty of time to think since, since — and I've decided what I'm going to do. I can work in Milan, just like I do here. Not in the fields — I don't suppose there are any near a city that big — but I can work as a maid or do laundry or cook in a school or remake mattresses — all those things, anyway, other women don't seem to want to do. And even if it costs us more to live, Pietro's making good money now and he won't have room and board to pay. Sometimes he sends home 60,000 *lire*, sometimes 70,000 *lire* ($95–$110) a month. We'll have that, plus what I make, and the children can go to better schools and Giuseppe can have his operations just the same. I've already asked the doctor in Bari. He gave me a name. So when Pietro comes home in August I'll tell him I'm going to Milan with him to find a place for us all to live and a job for me. Then I'll come back here and get the children." She stopped, but the tears still ran down her cheeks. I could think of nothing to say, so we sat that way in silence.

"If he doesn't want me to come," she finally went on, "I'll go somewhere else and work for all of us. I'm through here. I can't take anymore; I *won't* take anymore. Can you understand what I mean? Do you understand *why* I can't take anymore? Do you? No one is ever going to make me ashamed of being alive again. I'm *never* going to crawl down the street — *ever* again. Never, never, never as long as I live. Can you understand how I feel?"

I could. She and Pietro fought every night that August, but I could have told him nothing would change her mind this time. Just as she had said, she left with Pietro. When she returned ten days later, she packed up her belongings and her children and disappeared without a word to anyone.

I have never seen her since, though they tell me she came back, very well-dressed and rather superior, for a few days last summer. The first years she worked very hard at all those jobs she talked about, the ones other women did not want to do. The children finished school and found work. Giuseppe had his operations, is apparently normal, has a job and a girl he is "half-engaged" to, though his mother and father say he is too young to think of marriage. For the last ten years Pietro has worked in a huge food processing plant, is now a supervisor, and has too much seniority to suffer greatly from a recession. Ninetta no longer works; she stays at home in a small apartment they now almost own and is very much the Signora.

The first Christmas after she left, she sent me a Christmas card on which she had written just one phrase: *Solo i fessi stanno laggiù!* Only the fools stay down there!

"Sometimes I wonder what will happen when I'm not young anymore. I don't let myself think about it, except some nights my back hurts so bad I can't stay in bed, so I get up and go out to sit in the cool by the door. Then it just goes around in my head: What will happen to me? I've been a stonemason's helper before, when there wasn't work in the fields. It's all right as long as you're young, but it takes a lot out of a woman. I work from eight to six for 3,500 lire a day ($5.40) and no insurance. Whenever I can find a day's work I take it. You see I have five children, and my husband is in Germany. He's been there before — three times. He stays a year and then comes home and tries to find work here. They — the government, the politicians, you know — they keep promising jobs for everyone, but it's never true. When I was a girl — before I married — why, even then they were saying in five years, in ten years, and look at me. Anyway, my husband stays here until the money runs out, then he goes back. This time he's been up there two months and still no work, even there. Pretty soon he'll have to come home. My mother-in-law had a letter written to him saying I've disgraced him, that I have no modesty or I wouldn't go out to work like this, but maybe he'll understand. If I can feed us here, then he doesn't need to send us money, so he can stay longer and go on looking. I can do it for a while yet. All I hope is my children don't end up this way, but I don't really believe anything will be different."

Teresa

At times I felt as much a captive of the town as the true
Italian *confinato* who, at the request of the Prefecture, is
exiled to a remote village, preferably in the mountains,
for "crimes" not subject to formal prosecution, such as his
presence *near* the scene of a riot, or his friendship with
men *believed* to be planning some dastardly act. The law,
a convenient leftover from the Fascist statutes of public
safety, requires no proof, only suspicion and one elo-
quent statement by the Deputy Prefect to the court:
"Quest'uomo mi da fastidio." This man annoys me, or is
troublesome to me. For a year or two or sometimes even
more the *confinato* must stay within one kilometer of the
limits of his assigned village. I suffered from no such
prohibition, but I was not immune to the cloistral frustration of village life. Flight was the only remedy I ever
found, almost as though by leaving I proved to myself
that I was not yet a prisoner. I always did the same thing:
I picked up my cameras and drove off into the country.
Later I discovered everyone knew about my supposed

rendezvous with a traveling salesman, a gentleman in soap, I believe it was.

What they never knew was how much I learned from just sitting, watching a hillside or a narrow, private little valley or even one of the sweeping plateaus which open so unexpectedly and which, deceptive as the sea, appear to be without secrets. I stopped whenever some quirk of light or elephantine pleating of rocks and fields appealed to me. There was never anyone about, and so I am not sure, even today, whether people arrived on stage one by one, following some fortuitous cue, or whether like animals in the jungle, they had sensed an intruder and waited, immobile, until they could estimate the danger. My landscape was deserted. Then a faint click of metal hitting a rock made me look more closely at a vineyard. There, among the gnarled vines, was a woman dressed in black, raising a mattock over her head, pausing a fraction of a second, then hunching forward to concentrate her strength as she brought the blade smashing down into the dirt. When she straightened up, she would lever a clump of earth free, break it with the foot of her hoe, and then slowly raise the handle again. Closer to me, when the wheat shivered in a gentle breeze, I suddenly saw a woman bent over, moving along a row, weeding. Then a man, leading a donkey with water barrels strapped to the pack saddle, would appear on my left, plod slowly across my landscape until he disappeared on my right. I had only to wait, and he would eventually return, walking just as slowly, as blindly as before, like an automated toy jerking along in invisible track. So until twilight, the women, each at her own rhythm, will pound the mattock into unyielding clay or chop with her hoe down one row, up the next, while the man with his donkey trundles back and forth, carrying water.

One hot summer morning, in desperate flight, I drove out along the ridge behind the village and followed it until it dipped into a valley and out again onto a bald mesa. I had never stopped there, for it was only a vast, treeless expanse of stubble with the road, like a backbone, running down the middle. That morning I saw a girl with a hoe on one shoulder, far away to my left, leading two goats and three kids on ropes. Before they reached the falling off place and slowly disappeared, it seemed, into the rank grass, I took some pictures of them and then, having stopped, wondered what was below the blind edges. I went to the right through thistles, over tufted lumps of clay and into ditches, no deeper than troughs, disguised by luxuriant growths of nettles, until I stumbled onto a narrow path that meandered parallel to the road, then dipped sharply to the right and down. Below me, almost a ledge, was a long tongue of land checked with wheat fields. Some had been reaped, leaving others to stand like proud, isolated hedges. Even without walls, as they were, there was no doubt where one ended and another started; the earth, the plants themselves had assumed the personalities of the men who worked them. In some the soil lay in clots, as though it had not been harrowed, as though, at best, the peasant had reworked it with a hoe, and the wheat was sparse. In others the stalks were thick and so were the weeds. A dog-leg had been slashed in one where the wheat was singed a dead ocher and the ears rattled in the breeze. No one was in sight. Above the fields, just under the brow of the mesa, huddled a low stone house which might have been there, a victim of the weather's vandalism, for ten years or ten centuries. The chimney had collapsed into a jagged hole, and the sun had cleaved deep cracks in the bleached window frames where a generation of lizards now played hide and seek. The only signs of human occupants were a few scrawny, despondent chickens pecking at the hard dirt and a tree trunk whose foliage had been hacked off so that pots could be hung on the stumps of its limbs.

I peered through the long lens of my camera. Sheaves dotted the field with the dog-leg; they had not yet been stacked. Still I could see no one. There was no movement near the house, or in the fields, nor sounds except the grinding of cicadas and a faint swoop of the wind.

"What do you want?" said a surly voice.

A small, very muscular young man in a faded blue shirt and patched trousers had come up behind the rock on which I sat with my camera paraphernalia spread around me. His face, as unfriendly as his voice, was burned the color of well-stained walnut. It was extremely flat and wide with a long chin, high cheekbones and a small arched nose. He might have been an Indian except for his very small, sharp blue eyes and a bush of very curly black hair that did not quite twist into fuzz.

"I asked what do you want?" he repeated impatiently.

"Nothing. I just — well . . ." My voice trailed away in guilt and confusion.

"Must be spying with that thing, that . . ." He pointed at my camera. "Who for? The police? The Land Reform?"

I almost laughed, but he was serious — and irritated. I explained who I was, that I lived in town, ran a nursery there, up on the hill, that I was just interested in the countryside, in the farming, in the crop. How was the harvest this year? He was not to be distracted.

"Why do you want to know?"

"Who is it, Paolì?" A thin young woman with wide gentle brown eyes and a scarf wrapped around her head so that it came out over her forehead and cheeks almost like a bonnet had appeared behind the man's shoulder.

"She says . . ." and he repeated my explanation. She looked from him to me and smiled. She had no visible front teeth!

"Carlo goes to the nursery," she said and added to me, "That's my cousin's little boy." She turned back to Paolino. "She says the Signora is *tanto brava.*" If she were offering a recommendation, this apparently was enough.

"If that's who she is — really — then I guess it's all right, but you never know," he grumbled, then turned and sauntered away as though we were no longer of interest.

"Teresa Petruselli," she said, switching a sickle she held to offer me a limp, calloused hand. "He's my husband, Paolino, and behind that broom bush down there is our little girl. We were about to eat when he saw you. It's early, I guess, but we've been working since the sun came up. A long morning. You're welcome to join us, except . . ." and she hesitated. "Except we haven't much to offer, just *salame* and a bit of fried omelet, but there's plenty of wine." She did not bother to include the basis of their meal — bread. I thanked her, said I would sit with them for a while, even if I did not eat: I had not, after all, been working since dawn. She accepted that as an adequate explanation. In time I learned she is a very practical, straightforward woman who can be intimidated into nervous silence, but never wastes time cringing: "This bread is too coarse for you," or "This is *nothing* that you would ever eat," or "This hut we live in is not worthy . . ." are sham phrases that come automatically, too automatically, to many peasant women; to her, not at all.

When I had packed it, she took up my camera case and strode off ahead of me with that gait particular to very thin peasant women: pelvis forward, knees bent, as though like a leaf spring, she had been warped by weights too heavy. As we walked I noticed the curious combination of clothes she wore: a wild purple and orange shirt of a kind known locally as a *"camicia all'americana,"* a dusty dark green skirt which, to judge by the tracery of seams, both new and ripped out, had started life in some other capacity, tan wool knee socks and felt shoes, like Daniel Green bedroom slippers. In contrast, when we reached her, the little girl, Angela, was the epitome of summer elegance in a blue and white dress with a sailor collar, closed blue sandals with rubber soles and red bows at the ends of her long dark braids. Later Teresa told me that her work clothes were shirts her husband had discarded and old dresses made into skirts.

"I don't need many clothes, you know, and new things make such a difference to children." She was not feeling sorry for herself. Paolino had complained that she looked like a rag-picker and this was the practical explanation of why. She hoped I would understand.

The broom bush offered a small triangle of shade for us. The food, a large round loaf of bread, and one knife were spread on an immaculate dishtowel, the corners of which doubled as napkins. In my honor Angela was sent off to find a second glass and told to wash it. Nestled back in the wire-like reeds of the bush were a two-liter bottle of wine with a porcelain stopper and a large clay water jug with a long neck and two handles that made it look like a shrewish, but headless woman with her arms akimbo. We were perhaps two or three hundred feet below the edge of the mesa and whatever breeze there was did not reach us. We might have been in an enormous blue-domed furnace surrounded by wheat stalks that sang in the heat.

Conversation was not easy. Once Paolino had spread out his jacket, which he insisted I sit on, he concentrated with almost priestly devotion on laying out the food. Only a corner of the *frittata* remained, but there was one whole and a nubbin of another cigar-shaped *salame* and some peppers put up in oil. I asked about the children, a subject that offers little threat.

Although Teresa talked easily enough, she did not look at me. Instead she pleated and unpleated a corner of the towel, occasionally waving her hands in deprecatory little gestures of either dismissal or maidenly shyness, it was hard to tell. There were three children: two girls and a boy. The eldest was Angela, who, unlike her mother, fixed me with a hypnotic, wide-eyed stare of wonder and disbelief. She had finished the second grade, the little boy would start school the following year, though he was frail and subject to prolonged attacks of bronchitis, and the baby would go to nursery school.

"Now that there are schools, they've got to go as long as they can. I never really went myself — well," and a wave of the hand. "That is, I went for a little while and then there was the war and besides in those days no one sent a girl more than a couple of years, anyway. My father put me out to work. There were twelve of us, and he said if we were going to eat, we were going to have to work. Paolino's been to school though; he did all five grades. He knows how to read."

"Then he must write too," I said just to make an attentive noise.

Another little wave of the hand and a shake of her head. "He only remembers to sign his name. Those schools were different, not like the ones today, and then when you finished the one in town, there weren't any others for people like us. That's why the children have got to go. They can do anything if they have the right piece of paper." She stopped for several long minutes until I thought she would not go on, but she may just have been dreaming of her children as doctors, lawyers and professors. " 'Til after the war there weren't any nurseries either. Then they started saying it wasn't good for kids to be locked out in the street all day. Don't know what they expected," a flip of the hand and the pleating in the towel sprang apart. "What would you do if you had to work in the fields and didn't have a mother or a mother-in-law or somebody right by ready to take them? Now, she," she said, motioning toward Angela, "went to the nuns and you know what they did all day? They sang. Seems to me the earlier they start learning to read and write, the better it'd be. But, no, not the nuns. And every time I went to get her they were saying, '*Fate figli, fate figli!*' (Have children, have children!) 'til I quit going. The Party says there are too many; the nuns say not enough. What are you supposed to think? Little Nicola, I didn't send him. To tell you the truth they told me I *couldn't* send him because of politics, but I'd send Anna if I could find a place like I want, where they teach the children how to read and write. I don't know, maybe she could come to your nursery. You'd teach her to read and write, and everybody says they eat good up there and you don't have to send the food with them."

Paolino, who had been slicing bread with the loaf propped against his chest, stopped and rested his chin on the thick crust. This was the test. His very stillness emphasized the challenge, but I had no choice. As long as I controlled a nursery, no child would be taught to read and write, especially these children whose verbal and manual skills were so underdeveloped. As I explained to Teresa, it was more important for children to learn to express themselves in the language of the school — to them a mysterious language, Italian — and more important for them to have something as large as a paint brush or a crayon under control before they sat, niggling all day with a pen AAAA,aaaa,AAAA,aaaa,BBBB,-bbbb,BBBB,bbbb. I side-stepped the social development of the child in a nursery, which is equally important. To Teresa and Paolino a child who sees himself as one alone against the world has understood the fundamental law of survival. They would reject, as futile, the compromises he either learns, or is forced to make, if he is to endure the long years of schooling so hopefully planned by his parents.

Teresa was reluctant to postpone reading and writing. For her they were magic skills, the open sesame to a remote but entirely desirable world. Once when I knew her better, I asked why she did not go to the free evening schools where reading and writing and all the other subjects of the elementary grades were taught to men and women who, like her, had not gone to school. She seemed surprised, then amused at the idea.

"Why should I do that? It's no use to *me!* I can sign my name and that's enough. Just crowd my head with silliness. My life's settled. It's the way it is and that's all right. Imagine me, sitting there learning what a baby learns right after he knows to tell you he wants to go to the toilet, instead of doing it in his pants."

But that first morning her conviction was so strong that she was slow to see an advantage dangling from every sentence, like fruit before Tantalus. I liked her the better for her tenacity and could only listen in silent amusement and sympathy when, the fruit clearly in focus, she started tactical maneuvers to reach it. Paolino, who had returned to his bread, finished slicing and put the knife down. He watched us with narrowed eyes as Teresa went about plowing under her ideas, one by one, and could finally say with some grace,

"So really there is time enough to learn, I suppose, but all those other things you said — Italian and those things — you don't get them sitting, singing songs all day." She hesitated. "But it's not too late for Anna. Next year, you'd take her, wouldn't you?" She had arrived, and again there was only one answer I could give.

"I can't promise anything now . . ." The rest of what I would have said — about needier children or those who had no one at home to care for them — was lost in an angry spate of words from Paolino.

"You see! That's what I told you last night and you wouldn't admit I was right. Do you understand now? It's po-li-tics that control everything. I'll throw it in your face one more time: po-li-tics! She won't give you a place in the nursery, she won't do it, I tell you. We don't vote the right way. That one there," he went on, pointing to the little girl who still watched me, but now with blinking fear, "Why did the nuns send her away? Why? The same reason! What we think doesn't suit her. And why? Politics, po-li-tics! This damned land! Why do I have it, why do I have so little when others . . . ? I'll tell you: po-li-tics. It's the same with this one — she won't give you a place. She's already sniffed it, that we're Communists. And I say to both of you, I am and I'll stay one just as long as politicians give out land according to how a man votes, not what he needs, just as long as I can't get a job unless I vote the right way and just as long as those nuns say, '*Fate le brave, fate figli, fate figli!*'" He stopped and turning to me, added, "And I say it right in front of you. It's your fault and those other people like you, if my children starve. '*Fate figli, fate figli*' — and who's to feed them. ME. Not you! I've got a choice. I'm a young man, but I've got a choice: Watch my children starve, if we have any more; or go to whores. Which do you suggest? And I've got that choice just because your Church won't allow birth control pills to be sold. You're playing God, but you're doing it with MY life. You'll keep me from working, give me the crumbs of land that are going and send me to the whores too. Thanks, thanks a lot. Forget it, Teresa. You won't get a place for Anna from this one. Here, eat what you want. I'm going to the house." He stood up and never looking at either of us, motioned the little girl to come with him.

Teresa and I sat in silence for a few moments, she, still pleating and unpleating the corner of the towel, her eyes down. Then very quietly, without looking up, she said,

"Don't be angry with him. He's nervous and worried and he blows up like that, but he's a good man. It does seem sometimes that po-li-tics, like he said, run everything." She stopped and waited, using this mild apology as conversational litmus paper. I was not angry. I had no reason to be since I am neither Catholic nor a politician. Teresa would hardly have understood my real reaction: relief that finally one of those frustrated men had said what he thought, instead of whining and fawning.

As we talked, we began to eat — a slice of *salame*, a bit of pepper — not really hungry, but in unconscious obedience to Paolino. Teresa said he would come back in a while sorry for his anger and perhaps even able to apologize. Then she began to explain why he was so bitter. When the war ended, he was still a boy, but he listened to his father and his friends talk. What he understood was that every peasant was to have land of his own. It was inevitable, he told her, because the Communist Party promised that land would be expropriated from large landowners, the common enemy, and given to the peasants who, for once, could not lose. The Christian Democrats, the ruling Catholic party, had a choice to make: rebellion or some form of the same program. In the end she and Paolino were married before anything really happened. The reform bill was passed, and Paolino, who had no land and worked by the day for big landowners, knew *he* would be allotted land. But he had not calculated the house in the village, which had been Teresa's dowry. He had to do one of two things: he could see it and be assigned a house and five hectares ($12\frac{1}{2}$ acres) of land as yet unreclaimed and commit himself to a thirty year hire-purchase contract plus repayment of a certain percentage of reclamation costs and the charges for equipment used in normal plowing, sowing, and reaping; or if he insisted, he could keep the house and two hectares (five acres) of land would be "given" to him, again on hire-purchase, to farm.* It was a sop, he said, to make him toe the line. If he were not to be excluded entirely, he had to accept it, which he did, and then watched as men whose political opinions came prepackaged from the sacristy were allowed to keep houses, bits of land, even equipment and still appeared on the lists as the owners of new houses and reclaimed land from the agency. Politics, he said, just like his child not being acceptable to the nuns. Why? Because he did not want a squad of children he could not support, because his politics were not theirs. And They, which for Paolino meant every priest and nun, Bishop and Pope alike, were the basic cause of the South's overpopulation, the poverty, the jobless world that forced

* ". . . According to the provisions of the land reform act, the assignment of land is made with a contract of sale on instalments payable in thirty years, the land remaining the property of the Board until the payments have been completed.

"The sale price must not be greater than two thirds of the total cost of the improvement works carried out by the Board, on the farm free of the State contribution contemplated by the 1933 law on land reclamation for agrarian improvements, plus two thirds of the expropriation indemnity paid to the original owner. The rate of interest payable for the instalments is 3.5%. The instalments are arranged in such a way that the first two yearly payments are not subject to interest . . .

"The contract of sale is generally in the name of the head of the farmer family and the law forbids, until the full sale price has been paid, any arrangements of any kind whatsoever for the total transfer or partial use of the holding, which cannot be made the object of a mortgage, nor can be sequestered unless by or on behalf of the Board . . .

"The contract sale also obliges the assignee, in accordance with the law, throughout a period of twenty years from the date of signing the contract to participate in the co-operative societies or syndicates which the Board has engaged itself to promote or set up, with the object of guaranteeing technical, economic and financial assistance to the new land-owners."

Land Reform in Apulia, Lucania and Molise, prepared for distribution in English by the *Ente Riforma*, Bari, September 1963. Pages 29–30.

It should also be noted that if, through some windfall, a family was able to pay its total indebtedness before the thirty year period expired, it was forbidden to do so. [A.C.]

men to leave their own country if they wanted to survive. The prepackaging he recognized in the politics of others eluded him in his own: personal or party line, the important element was that it made sense to him. And Teresa, I wondered, did she agree? I asked her and for a moment thought she was going to escape with the Southern woman's usual excuse: Politics are for men.

"Beh, sometimes I think he goes too far, but then, so often things work like he says that I guess I do really. Anyway I always vote like he does. We talk about it and then do the same thing, because if I didn't and I chose to vote for the opposite thing, it'd be like neither of us went to vote at all and that's wrong. But I still go to Church. I won't give that up, and he knows it. *He* is the one who wants the children to be baptized. It's funny, but it's true. It's very important to him. He's superstitious about it."

We wandered into birth control. She did not know that even though the government-run houses of prostitution no longer existed, condoms were sold in all pharmacies. She thought about that for a minute and decided Paolino would not approve of them: they were for whores. She knew there was a Church-approved method, but no one had ever explained how it worked. Leaving aside any question of dependability or human variations in cycles, Ogino-Knaus, as a system, is relatively simple, if, and only if, I found out, a course in elementary biology is somewhere in the background. I had learned nothing from trying to explain the solar system to Chichella and if this time I did not end up with apples, oranges, lemons and all the tomatoes from the storeroom strewn over the kitchen table, gyrating, according to me, on various logical axes, my new pupil had the same bewildered look and a sheaf of incomprehensible drawings covered with arrows and blips and figures. It seemed best to skip on, hiding behind that Olympian immunity of, "Well, it's complicated, but that's the way it works. And the pills are based on the same cycle, only it's — it's different." I saved myself again. I did say that they were sold in Italy, that they seemed safe enough. Recently a national popular magazine had published enormous pictures of all the brands' boxes, which seemed almost an invitation to be your own doctor. Where all this might have ended I do not know because just then Paolino called to us.

"Did you leave me anything to eat?" He was walking down the hill, holding Angela by the hand.

He mumbled something about sorry his temper had run away with him and started eating bread, while Teresa reported on all, or almost all, we had talked about. He nodded absently as he stuffed slices of *salame* in his mouth and then took a long drink of wine and more bread, nodding the whole time. When he was wiping his mouth on the towel, which Teresa was waiting to wrap around the bread, he finally said,

"So you're not one of those *'fate figli'* ladies. Good! While Angela and I were up at the house I remembered someone complaining about how you refused to help people get houses, that you just brushed the recommendations away. It would have made me mad too, if I'd wanted a house, but if recommendations aren't right for jobs, I guess they're not right for houses — or places in the nursery either." His voice was so calm, so matter-of-fact, that this seemed almost a continuation of a conversation. "Now we've got to get back to work," he announced.

He pulled a leather apron out from behind the bush where he must have dropped it before they settled down to eat and slipped the bib strap over his head, hooked the sides around in back of him and then brought from his pocket four bamboo "thimbles," finger guards, and a leather thumb sheath, all of which went on the fingers of his left hand to protect them from the slashing of the sickle in his right hand. Because the apron was rigid and tended to trip him, he walked stiff-legged across the field, holding his fingers in the air so as not to lose his thimbles and his right hand with the sickle well out from his body to avoid spearing the apron. He looked like a mechanical monster from an early horror film, but once he bent to slice the wheat stalks and place them in the crook of his left arm, there was a grace in his movements that no machine, no matter how well-oiled, could ever imitate. Teresa worked behind him, taking the bundle from his left arm exactly at the moment when less would be too little, more too much. She divided the stalks, turned the heads of one half to meet the bottoms of the other and finally with a quick twist around and around she bound them with a few of their own stalks, dropped her sheaf and reached for the next armload. The heat was suffocating. It burned through the rope soles of my shoes and pierced my lungs. It felt like needles in my ears and all I did was walk along with them, taking a picture now and then. They ignored it, though Teresa was very red in the face and pulled her scarf further and further forward, trying to find even a splinter of shade. Still they went on: cut and cut and cut and hand over the bundle, and cut and cut and cut and hand over the bundle, each cut a sweep forward and a pull back in, each bundle a scoop, divided, swing end to end and wrap and wrap and wrap and drop.

I stayed for at least an hour, unwilling to admit that

there was thunder in my head and that the world around me was iridescent. It was Teresa who first noticed that my legs were scratched and bleeding from the razor edges of the wheat stalks. I never admitted that they stung and throbbed.

"We shouldn't have let you come down here with us. You have no stockings on. Don't you know you can't go into a wheat field without wool stockings? Look at mine. I'll take you up to the well." She motioned to Paolino. "He'll get along without me for a while. It's just slower." Before she could tell him where we were going, Angela had stepped into her place and taken the next armload. Teresa smiled. "She knows how, but she can't do it for too long. Come on."

At the house she made me take my shoes off and then threw several buckets of cold water on my legs, talking all the while about how when she was "younger" she used to bind for four men at a time.

"And I got a man's wages for it, but it about killed me. There, that'll help for a while. When you get home, do it again. Now come in our room for a few minutes. We can get out of the heat."

"Our room" was the lean-to at the end of the house with a dirt floor and no window. Inside the only furniture was a broken-down cot, one corner of which was held up by stones, and a three-legged wooden stool. Scythes and axes, hoes and shovels and picks and mattocks were propped with their handles in a jumble against the wall. Bits of harness hung on nails over sacks of feed where two chickens had roosted and were now gazing at us with alarmed yellow eyes. Here over the years we have talked about a little bit of everything. I went only once to their house in the village. Three steps below the level of the street, it was neat and bare and dank, a cave where no light penetrated unless the door was open. She sent to the neighbors for a chair for me and made some coffee she took from a twist of brown paper. Her stove was a two-ring burner which she had bought, secondhand, as a great bargain. She was not at ease there, as she was in the lean-to above their fields. It lacked nothing convention decreed it should have, whereas the house, I think, made her feel poor and drab.

Here, in the lean-to, mending sacks or sorting beans or braiding little Anna's hair, for she talked very little if she did not have some chore to keep her hands busy and her eyes averted, she told me about her life. Unlike Paolino, she did not see the world as scheming against either of them. Trials and disappointments were a normal part of life, and if she accepted them with stoic resignation, it was because she knew that someday she and Paolino would prosper. That was the pattern of the world. She did not recognize her own paraphrase of God's will, or the penances one must endure to arrive at a state of grace. This was not the well-worked mold of Catholic orthodoxy; this was grim practicality: life could hardly worsen, so it must improve. In the meantime failure followed hope with metronomic regularity.

She was a clever mimic, but shy about it, and I learned that as long as she made the effort to speak something resembling Italian, garbled as it was, our conversations would be entirely formal. When finally she relaxed and slipped without noticing it into dialect, her imagination could slip loose too. Naturally she saved her talent for those she disliked. Her gentle, low voice would harden and the words she used were suddenly those her victims would inevitably have chosen, but with all the mincing sarcasm of her scorn to make them ridiculous. It was a treatment she reserved for all teachers, her own parish priest who had made some untoward gesture to Angela, she thought, and for most politicians. She mocked their gentility, their hypocrisy and their double-talk, but true venom was aimed at unctuous nuns. She would stick out her stomach and waddle around the room, wringing her hands, slowly intoning,

"Ah, my children, my poor children. I feel for you. Never fear, God will provide. *He* will provide. Don't ask me, I am but His humble servant. Ah, my poor children, my poor children!" She would stop, put her hands on her hips and say in a dead voice, "Sure, 'My poor children,' but make *sure* your parents vote the right way!"

She loathed her doctor's wife, a determinedly gen- teel lady who always wore tight corsets, tighter dresses and very high heels which made her literally "ankle" through the Piazza, the only public place she was ever seen. "Ah my sainted husband, for he is a saint," Teresa had all the syrup of the woman's voice and the fluttery little motions of her hands that accompanied the nonstop expression of her deepest thoughts. "He is sacrificing himself, li-ter-ally sacrificing himself for his beloved poor. Sometimes I wonder, And what of me? Yes, what of me? For him it's a mission. But he'll kill himself. Yes, he is a sainted man. So good, so unselfish, so devoted to his mission. Yes, his mission. He's sacrificing himself!" Te- resa would stop dead. *"Uffa, mi fa nausea!* Sure, he's sacrificed himself, right into a villa at the sea, a new house in town, half of which he rents to the tax collector, he's foreclosed on four farms this year and still people bor- row from him — there's no one else. He sacrifices himself all right! He sleeps through the hours when you're supposed to be able to see him free on the insurance, but he never misses his private office hours, so in the end we all have to pay — and listen to *her* while we wait. That's sacrifice, is it?"

Of them all it was Angela's teacher who exasperated Teresa the most. Often a teacher starts the first class with the children and moves up with them each year until they finish the fifth. It can be a very happy arrangement, or a tragic one, depending on the teacher: in Angela's case it was tragic. The teacher was very young, preferred boys, if possible of good family, talked very fast in class and would not tolerate questions because, she said, they interrupted her train of thought. She had also, apparently, taken against Angela. Whether or not Teresa realized it, each time she went to ask about Angela the same scene took place. Eventually I did not follow every word of her re-enactments, but was always reminded that parents were expected to consign their children for four hours daily without right of questions or advice.

"You see this time," Teresa would say, "I promised myself that I'd get some satisfaction from her. I'd find out at least why she dislikes Angela so. I took some beans" (or apples, or chestnuts — whatever was in season) "in a basket and just like last time, it was enough that she saw me. She started yelling at me — 'I don't have the time. You can't expect me to drop everything and worry about your precious Angela. No no, signora. I'm obliged to put up with *her* during hours, but not with *you*. Besides what can you understand about school? You can't even read.'" Teresa's voice had the high sharpness of the teacher's and the cadence, but the large words that always came next defeated her. "'It's pedalogically pointless to discuss her with you. What can you understand about her ration of apprenticeship' (which I decipher as her rate of learning) "or her composture. You can't expect miracles, signora. You're ignorant. We will do our best with your little girl, but you mustn't expect too much. Here, give me the basket.' And you know, she takes the basket each time and never gives it back. Just slams the door in my face and leaves me there like a thief with people gaping at me from the street."

At times her asperity was so out of proportion with the importance of the people in her life, so at variance with her public and apparently natural temperance that I found myself wondering, not entirely to my credit perhaps, if she were a very deceptive actress, if, in fact, she were a "secret" virago. The human being is seldom consistent, but it is impossible for him to be consistently what he is not. I have now known her almost fifteen years. I have seen her children run to her with all kinds of news — ranging from a worm they have found to a slap someone has given them — which they would not have done if she were normally irritable or cruel with them. Once when I looked for her in town her neighbors said she would not be back from the fields until late. One woman volunteered,

"She works for ten. Comes home *zitta, zitta* (quiet, quiet), leaves *zitta, zitta,* her house and her children clean. Sometimes we don't see her for days, but, when we do, she's always got a smile and a word for everyone. If you want to leave a message, we'll give it to her — but no telling how soon."

A rare panegyric in Southern Italy! I have watched her bargaining in the market, waiting her turn at the hospital, grieving and hoping and discouraged. I am convinced she is a moderate, fatalistic woman, gentle by nature, who is naive enough to accept the outside world on faith as all good, but is astute about her own to the point of misanthropy, at least about what she calls "those who command." She never mimics anyone else.

She and Paolino were married as soon as he finished his military service.

"From the time we were little things everyone knew we would," she said proudly. "We did too. It never occurred to me that I might marry someone else — just never went through my head." As it would never have occurred to her that she might choose not to marry at all. There are no peasant spinsters. They cannot afford such whims and the convents, which were their only refuges from suitors repulsive to them but acceptable to their families, are ever less appealing. Husbands are obligatory for women as wives are utilitarian for men. Physical charms may attract a more eligible young man, one, say, who has a mule rather than a battered bicycle, or works as an unskilled laborer in Germany rather than hopes for next spring's building season, but the strength of youth has its own value that transcends beauty, and attraction is incidental. Women's liberation is a phrase without meaning: marriage remains a duty as holy as any of the Commandments.

Teresa was one of twelve children, the only girl who survived, and so her maternal grandmother's house had been kept for her dowry. Paolino was one of six. Both families owned strips of land here and there which, if they could have been combined, would not have covered the town piazza. Each child had to make his own way, and they did, as unskilled laborers in the construction boom that followed the war, or as tenant farmers. A few went to Milan or Germany, but without notable success. They came home quickly.

Before Angela was born in 1952, Paolino was confident of a new house and land from the Land Reform partly because, though it sounds paradoxical, he was active in the Communist Party. "One of the belligerent ones because they're the ones who are respected," Teresa said, echoing a boast of Paolino's, his daily litany in which she never put much faith. "One of the belligerent ones because they can't be put aside." And by implication the ones whose silence would be most valuable to the Christian Democratic Party. Blackmail was no secret. Disguised as democratic impartiality, it was offered and accepted with greedy enthusiasm. The same men who threatened and blustered in public and showed signs of becoming leaders other peasants would follow, were castrated by their own cleverness. The Land Reform had bought and paid for their cooperation: should an unwise "assignee" become recalcitrant, it was easy enough to remind him not just of his moral debt to the *Ente Riforma*, but of his very tangible debt for his hire-purchase contract, his fertilizer, his seed, insecticides and the tractor and services he had used at so much a day. For all his cunning the peasant had maneuvered himself into the ambiguous position of being an indentured land owner and worse, his master was no one man but the hydra of modern civilization, a government agency.

Some innate caution made Teresa and Paolino refuse to give up their little house where the floors never dried and no amount of sun and air could defeat the inroads of mildew. Paolino said that even without water or plumbing a house in town would always have *some* value. Teresa had nothing to say for the house itself, but did not think she would be changing for the better if she accepted a house, even a new one, in the country, isolated from all other human beings, without light and water, which had been promised "immediately." She knew better than to trust in such promises.

(She was right. Ten years later those same houses still had no light, and water had to be carried from the nearest fountain, sometimes a mile or more away. What she could not have imagined was that those original houses, made of prefabricated plaster panels, began to show dangerous cracks. Walls were braced with thick iron rods, set diagonally from corner to corner, forming an "X" that hung over one's head like an omen of disaster. In many cases the houses had to be entirely replaced. Ultimately what the "assignee" had paid on the first house was allowed as part payment of his debt on the second house, which was, however, much more expensive and so put him further in the hole to the Land Reform.)

Teresa and Paolino kept their house and accepted a plot of land originally intended to integrate a small peasant holding into a self-sufficient farm. On that long narrow plateau they were allotted two hectares (five acres). Two other men were assigned a hectare apiece. The house, though it belonged to no one of them and technically must have been the property of the Land Reform, fortunately had three rooms of roughly equal size and dilapidation, which they appropriated as storerooms. Teresa kept chickens there and so was committed to regular trips from town. During periods that require the most work, she often slept there with the donkey and a child or two to save herself the long walk back to town and out again the following morning.

Soon enough they realized the land might feed them

a meager diet, but it produced little in the way of salable crops, even if they were willing to go hungry. An offer to pay the electricity bill with so many days' work might amuse the clerks in the regional office, but the light would be cut off just the same. The clothes merchant, the textbook seller and the grocer looked on barter with the same scorn. Every family needed some actual, printed money. The fall after their first crop Paolino left for Germany. He had intended to stay, Teresa said, until the plowing was done, but that year summer never came to an end. There was no rain and so no hope of planting. Teresa plowed the land with a borrowed mule and a wooden plow: the share itself was the trunk of a hefty tree hacked to a point and strengthened by a metal tip, like a dunce cap.

"Yes," she admitted, "the Land Reform could have plowed deeper, but we already owed them so much we had no way to pay, and besides our land is like a little island away from the big tracts, so they never come to us until the very end, sometimes when it's already too late. That's fair when there are so many plots that can be worked together, but we pay the same rate, you know. It wasn't so bad. I did it slow." She stopped and smiled wistfully, as though remembering that year. "I was younger then," she finally went on. "That was the year — no, maybe it was the next. I don't remember, except that I plowed both years. Anyway, whichever year it was, just before I'd decided to cut the wheat, I mean like the day before, a hailstorm knocked it all flat on the ground and ruined it. You know how, after one of those storms, everyone who isn't already in the fields gets out on the road as fast as they can to see if anything happened to their crops. The roads are full of people and they all talk like they were cheerful, but I know how *I* feel. My heart pounds and I keep thinking I'm going to be sick. That time I found it all lying on the ground and chewed looking. I came in here and sat and cried for hours. Every time I felt a little better and started to do something — I don't know, mix the feed for the chickens — I'd look out that door and see the fields again and I couldn't help it — I'd cry."

In Germany Paolino had tried, but never found regular work. He held out on two days work one week, three, the next when he could get it, and finally late in November, when he had spent the money he had brought with him and most of what he had earned, he bought his ticket and came home. The next spring and summer he worked up north in a tunnel for premium wages. Teresa said when he came back, he looked like an old man.

"Every morning he went in there to work, he about wet his pants he was so scared. He swore he would starve before he went back. One year he tried Turin, but things went just so-so. He sent home a little. Everything helped. Then there was some place near Florence, but I don't remember the name. He had some relatives who said they could get him a job. They did, but he found out he wasn't being paid right and they were getting a cut. He could have had a job on the railroad. Two winters he did that, 'til they offered him a real job with insurance and pension and everything, but he said when he had the night shift — that was half the time — in the winter, it was so cold and wet out and you couldn't see anything, you didn't know what was right there in front of you — maybe a live wire, maybe a washout. There were wolves too, when it was real cold, and there those men were walking the line, or if it wasn't their shift, lying on their bunks in the car on the siding. I told him to put the pillow over his head, so he wouldn't hear the wolves, but he said that didn't work. Maybe he tried it, but I'm not so sure, because he said there was always a light burning in there, and he wouldn't want the others to see him.

"Maybe I should have gone with him, but they wouldn't have let him be home much, and I had rent to pay and no one knew me. I saw it different and I still do. To me my job is to see this land gets farmed, to raise up the children, make them go to school and teach them what's right and get work, as much work as I can get while I'm still young enough to work in the fields, because that's all I know. I can do that here where people know I'm good help, where I know how to get around and I don't pay rent. Nobody can ever say Paolino didn't get on because he had a lazy wife! Some days I wish I could add. I bet if you count what I've got off the land and the chickens and those years I've had a pig and all my hired work, why, I bet I've brought in more in the last ten years than Paolino has, that is, money we could spend or food we could eat. Good years he's earned it, but he had to spend it too."

And so Paolino comes and goes. Some years are good, others bad, but he does not "get on," as Teresa put it. His dark face is dour now. Everything about it seems to turn down and a scowl has left permanent pleats between his eyebrows. These days politics do not interest him. All politicians are thieves: what Italy needs is the atomic bomb to set it right. Whoever is left can start again and make something of it — maybe.

Teresa is thinner, more stooped. The crow's feet at the corners of her eyes are with her winter and summer now, deep and white against the perpetual tan of her cheeks. Now there are five children. Angela married a "temporary" postman who should, someday, become permanent. Anna, the little girl who might have come to the nursery, has never done a day's work in the fields and never will, if her mother has her way. And she jeers at Teresa because she is stupid, a *cafona*, Anna calls her, no better than an animal. Nicola may be able to pass his examinations as a bookkeeper: probably not, but I do not talk to Teresa about it, for it makes no difference. There are hundreds of thousands of unemployed bookkeepers in Italy. It is too soon to know what the younger ones will do, except that they too will jeer at Teresa and be ashamed of her. For them she is a mindless drone. She disapproves of see-through blouses and rock dancing and girls going off with boys to films.

I am sure they do not know what she told me the last time I saw her. It was just before the referendum on divorce. Paolino was home, had been for most of the winter. When I met him on the road one morning, he lectured me about the destruction of the Christian family.

"If the politicians have their way, a woman could wake up one morning, take a look at her husband and decide to go off and leave him. Just like that — maybe even for another man. *Figurati!* There'll be nothing sacred left. But I'll tell you a secret, signora, these women are too smart for that. They *know* when they're well off: when they're married. No two ways about it!"

That morning I stopped near the little stone house and walked down that meandering path. Teresa was there. She took me into their one room, which still has the dirt floor and the sacks with the chickens roosting on them. She had hung an old lace curtain at the door which was, at the moment, tied back with string, making a deep swag between us and the fields. The sun filtered through the curtain made them seem distant, part of an imaginary land far, far away. We sat side by side on the old cot, looking out through the curtain, and talked for a while, but I knew cool, sunny days are precious and did not want to stay too long. At my first restless movement, she jumped up to hunt for the two ritual eggs. I would never take more; she has never agreed to less. As she gave them to me, she put her hand on my arm and said,

"Do you know what I'm going to do? I'm going to vote for the divorce. Not that my vote will do any good. It'll cancel Paolino's, all right, but I won't tell him. No matter what the Pope says I don't think a woman has to live with one mistake her entire life. For a man it's different. He leaves his wife and children and he finds another woman — just like that — but it's not that easy for us. We've got the children and all that. If we find some man who'll be good to us, everybody calls us whores — but for the man it's different, it's all right. If we got deserted and could put ourselves right with the law, then we'd have a lot better chance of a new life. Maybe we could be happy too. I'm not wrong, am I?"*

Of these women Teresa may be the least adventurous. She herself would only claim to be practical: to choose drudgery, no matter how practical, requires a certain courage and determination. Permanent work was the promise of Northern cities. If Paolino were no more fortunate than he had been in other projects, as hap-

* Lucania is one of the few regions that voted against the divorce law (53.6% against, 46.4% for), in spite of Teresa and many others like her.

pened, she would bear most of the financial weight. She knew no city skill. She did know how to wrench the most from the village in which she was born. It is easy to brand her as lacking initiative, as having no desire to "get ahead," that concept which seems so naive to the cynical people of the Mediterranean who, when they seek change, are driven by desperation not ambition. They do not expect to conquer the world: they try to increase their minimum. Their hopes are not for themselves, but for their children, and even then are not elaborate. They dream of them as government clerks, bookkeepers, nursery teachers, that lowest level of tyrants who bedevil a peasant's life. They would settle for permanent jobs for them in a factory with all the concomitant side benefits of money, security, and some mysterious standing in that they are modern slaves rather than prehistoric ones. Of this generation few peasant children, girls or boys, have ever worked in the fields. Well on their way to the false gentility of the half-educated, dressed in cheap versions of last year's fashion, they loiter on the roads and in the piazzas or listen to the latest pop songs. In the winter they let four hours a day pass in school; in summer those same four hours slip by anywhere but in the fields, and their parents approve, even though in twenty years they have watched hundreds of neo-clerks remain unemployed, lounging their lives away until they are offered a job appropriate to their pretensions. Often they never are. As outsiders we endow the family that emigrates with initiative even though their logical expectations are limited to a place on the welfare rolls of the chosen city, an art which incidentally Southern peasants have mastered in their own villages and have only the vaguest idea of how to arrange in a large city. (Northern Italians say they learn soon enough.) We insist on our motivations which are not theirs. Sometimes those who stay are more tenacious, not yet convinced the world should provide a better living for less work. I think they are less desperate, but not necessarily less resourceful.

Teresa chose the sure thing, but she should not be despised or misjudged for it. She guaranteed the family minimum and the relative security of the children, neither of which Paolino ever managed to do outside the village. These are the justifications she offers in public. They are acceptable, which is extremely important. Once I even heard her say that Paolino had ordered her to stay, which I know is not true: quite the contrary. Later she explained that it seemed the easiest explanation since no one would expect a wife to disobey her husband. I think there is another, more private reason for her insistence.

Teresa always called Paolino, with rather acid good humor, "*Un gran chiacchierone*," which *The Cambridge Italian Dictionary*, forsaking its usual elegance, defines as a great "gas-bag." Qualities which were once assets — his outspokenness, his cunning, his arrogance — have been magnified by each failure until they are active liabilities. For Paolino everything is short term — his enthusiasms, his shrewdness, his temper, his loyalties and his jobs. He has not so much looked for work as for an easy way to beat the system. He does not admit, probably even to himself, that he chose situations beyond his range, and so with each defeat his rancor and sense of persecution have grown. Today he is a very unpleasant man to live with: his bitterness sours the lives of those around him. He still reels off the advantages of abandoning the house and the land and moving the entire family to the North: they have almost exclusively to do with his comfort. Teresa's face is always noncommittal, her answers bland, but she said once,

"You see, he's so preoccupied with getting even that he's forgotten me and the children and all the practical things. Sometimes I can't stand it. I run out of the house just to get away from him and then I crawl in bed at night and pretend he's not there. That hatred he carries around with him, that terrible hatred! It makes every room too small until I can't stand it."

I think she found a way to give herself space, one which she can defend publicly with all those acceptable reasons: the house, the land, the children.

Odd that we insist that "simple" people, poor people, do not feel deep, continuous emotion. We allow them animal explosions of rage or passion or illogical exuberance and then dismiss them as too insensitive to suffer from the more subtle miseries, the psychological peas that we, the princes and princesses of a more intellectual world, must endure. We have a lot of time for rambles through our psyches. We tell each other about them — in excruciating detail — or we pretend we would not give ourselves away for the world, while we long for the relief of boring someone. In the end I suspect it is not a matter of our feeling more, but rather that we have more verbal facility and more time to kill, for we have to do less to stay alive. Frustration is a nagging presence in a human life almost beyond explanation to another person. It has no beginning and no foreseeable end. Action does not necessarily cure it: inaction leaves it sitting there in your head like a large blob of dough that slowly grows with the yeast of events, until the mind is numbed by a dull, aching desperation. We meet it in our own separate ways. Teresa chose and then worked for peace and what security she herself could provide. That she succeeded is no mean accomplishment for any woman — or any man.

"Nothing's private in a one-room house. The street's your second room, so the neighbors know when the sheets need mending again and how ragged your underwear is and when you fight with your husband and — like today — when you 'pare' your feet. No way to do it inside where nobody'd see you. It's too dark. Nothing's private, but that doesn't mean you get used to it. You don't!"

"I had nine children in that room, back there, and I suppose I'll die there the same way — with all the men in the family sitting around the fire, muttering, 'Why doesn't she hurry up about it.' When my time came and the pains started, I'd send my husband to call my mother — after she died, he called my sister — whichever it was would tell the midwife, and they'd come and stand by the bed and wait to see how far apart the pains were. I'd hear the shuffling in the room and know the men were arriving, one by one. My father, my brothers, my husband's brothers, they all sat there by the fire and drank wine and waited. If you make a sound, if a pain catches you by surprise, or the baby won't come out and you can't stand it and you moan, you've disgraced yourself. You keep a towel shoved in your mouth, and everytime it hurts so bad, you bite down on it and pray to God no noise comes out. I always tied a knot in one end so I could bite real hard, and my sister had a way of crooning and stroking me that made it better.

"I suppose I'll die the same way. The men used to say, 'She's a brave one, she is.' But I'll never forget the pain. I remember all nine times, just how they felt — and every one is different, I can tell you — and you just lay there and bite the towel and never let out a sound. Not once. So many times it was all for nothing too. Six of mine died. I could have wailed then — that's all right — but there are some hurts that stay inside. Every time one of my babies was about to be born I'd think to myself, You're going to die! This time, you're going to die! Then it'd come out. Somehow — I don't know how to explain it — but somehow it was like I had been born again. Maybe that's what gives a woman strength when she finds out she's pregnant. At least some part of her will go on. I tried to think of that when I wanted to scream. Nothing's private here, not birth, not death, not anything. No matter what anyone says though, you never get used to it."

POSTSCRIPT Now many peasant women have their babies at the hospital, or at least they have *one* there. Often they refuse to go back a second time. The young midwife assigned to the hospital, who has time for only a small outside practice, told me once that peasant women feel less pain and suffer less from what they do feel than "other women"— a nice bit of medical snobbery which assumes that either peasant sensitivity is blunted by work, or there is some mystical ratio between nerve ends and socioeconomic class heretofore unrecognized. I have always wondered if she understood anything of the peasant woman's strict code of behavior or of the shame she brings on herself if she flails about in pain. To her the shame is a brand as conspicuous, as permanent as a strawberry birthmark or a scarlet letter. She feels and remembers every cramp, every searing barb that has plucked at her spinal column and made her writhe, those same cramps and barbs that "other women," more pampered and more complaining, have mercifully forgotten. And too the young midwife probably never thought of the delivery "thrones," facing each other in one communal delivery room, as the final indignity a modern world could force upon innately modest women. So the stolid peasant woman half lies, half sits, her knees held high and splayed out by leather slings in the most humiliating position medicine has yet invented. She is fortunate if she is alone. Usually at least one other "throne" is taken, often all three. There, in silence, they wait, trussed up like prisoners in a medieval torture chamber, their teeth clamped firmly on those clean white towels they brought from home and their heads turned aside that they may neither see nor be seen. Down the way in separate cubicles their more sensitive sisters groan and cry out for painkillers.

I was in that communal delivery room only once, at the insistence of the midwife.

"You know all of them. They'd love a visit. It will help them pass the time," she had said. It seemed improbable, but I went with her.

As we opened the door two of the women hid their faces with their arms, the third pulled the towel over hers and I fled, remembering what the older woman "paring" her feet had said to me: "Nothing's private here, not birth, not death, not anything. No matter what anyone says though, you never get used to it."

Pinuccia

What parents or children may think of the *scuola dell'
obbligo* (the first eight years of school) is not important,
for it is what its name implies — obligatory. If asked, the
children shrug. It is something to endure, not to think
about, not to like or dislike. The parents will say it is a
good thing because there are no jobs now for anyone
who does not have "that piece of paper." Some talk
about "civilized people," that they must be educated: the
skill is less useful than the piece of paper. Others are
more openly ambitious. "My children must not work as I
have. There are schools now. They can be teachers, or
bookkeepers, or surveyors." The same parents would
rather feed and clothe their children, letting them drift
through drab years, than have them stoop to the physical
labor that has been the family curse. They can, at least,
be proud that their children are above such work.

Peasants have chosen their models from those
around them who appear to succeed, those who con-
descend to regulate the minutiae of daily existence. The

all-enveloping bureaucracy of the government offers safety with the chance to arrange, not be the victims of imbroglios. It also offers a certain social position which, though not lofty, requires the automatic civility the parents have never enjoyed. And, at the end of life, there is a pension. They are reaching for the possible, and the school, that piece of paper, is the means.

Because it is so important, they have definite opinions about the school, especially the mothers who watch and hear and resent the half-measure of each school day. Who would listen to them? No one — and besides, there is danger in criticism.

Four hours a morning or afternoon belong to the school. To provide the number of cubic centimeters of "air" deemed vital for each child, the classrooms have the general dimensions and acoustics of a squash court. It is a sweet-sour touch of grandiosity when scarcity imposes two shifts. Some ministerial rule of thumb says that, if the building is old, the desks should be new and vice versa, so formica and tubular metal units wobble and clatter on uneven brick floors, while splintery bench-desks with their writing surfaces furrowed by generations of pupils diligently chiseling away with their pens, sit squarely on greenish-white tile floors. The room will have the brief attention of a janitor or janitress, who sweeps up the old football pool tickets, shopping lists and cigarette butts around the teacher's desk and lines up the desks once more, creating the dusty, abandoned order of station waiting rooms.

The children shamble in wearing the leftovers of the family wardrobe, clothes that might keep them warm and were not needed by the others. Some who suffer from chronic ooze of yellow matter from their noses have their heads swathed in wool scarves. Others shuffle along in rubber boots so worn that their naked toes stick out the tips. When finally they sit down, the raggle-taggle gypsy look is camouflaged by rusty black smocks with white plastic lace collars. Reforms come, reforms go, but the black *grembiule* remains inviolate. A few regularly forget to wear theirs and a few wait month after month for the School Aid Committee to give them one. It becomes a point of honor on all sides. Each morning the teacher shouts out the rule requiring the smock, and so the day begins. Attendance is taken, a few remarks about homework, more often than not untouched by children who live in houses with one bulb hanging in the center of a single room, and then problems are put up on the blackboard.

Conditions remain remarkably static in the elementary schools of Southern towns. Once the pupils are more or less occupied, the women teachers settle down to plan dinner, writing out the shopping list. The men collect in the hall for a cigarette and send the janitor to the nearest café to bring back coffee — after making sure the director has left. If he has, they can count on him to stay away for at least two hours: he has a number of small farms worked by tenants and is convinced that peasants will not work unless supervised. The teachers have plenty of time to read the newspapers. Everything takes time. All compositions and problems are done twice — the *brutta copia*, a marked-up first draft, and the *bella copia*, a final, clean version. It is a doubling-up that conditions the mind for life, but in school it helps the hours to pass. From one class a little girl is sent off with the list of the teacher's chores; from another, a boy, one who, as the teacher would say, will not profit from class, but who knows how to ingratiate himself, will spend the rest of the morning running for cigarettes, taking messages, even marketing for his teacher's wife. That is the best. He may have a chance to steal some fruit off a vendor's counter.

Days, five years of them, trip one after the other, varied only by the local religious ceremonies or the chance arrival of a Minister, which requires the mobilization of the school children, two by two, in long snake lines to swell whatever collected multitude.

Late in the winter of 1972 I asked eight children I have known since they were born to come to see me, bringing their school books with them. They were all in the first class. Their parents have had little schooling and most have forgotten how to read or write anything other than their names, which in practice is all they are ever asked to do. The fathers of those eight children have spent a total of thirty-six years in Germany. The mothers have stayed at home, taking care of these children who continue to be born with alarming regularity.

The children came, some suddenly timid, others echoing what their mothers had probably said: "Do we get a candy?" They did and then showed me their composition books filled with neat pages of A's, B's and C's. No one admitted to enjoying those endless rows of letters; one said words were better. Further on they had reached syllables, neat rows of them, which never became words. They were exercises to show the adjustments which are necessary to maintain the original sound of consonants as they are followed by the various vowels. Each child read me the next day's lesson. There were three different texts being used in as many sections of the first grade. (Teachers are free to choose texts from an "approved" list and usually do so on the basis of which salesman offers the largest "premium.") They shared certain similarities — brightly colored pictures of things outside the experience of mountain children — a little girl chasing a butterfly, which boys and girls alike said was stupid, a sailboat which one boy refused to believe could be a boat at all, and an airplane one girl said could not be one because it was a plain old bus with wings. The texts used very long words which invariably hit the end of the line and so had to be hyphenated. The children's concentration as they read out loud was an actual physical strain: their little bodies quivered with tension. The index fingers pressed so hard under each printed syllable that the nails turned white and the lit-tle voi-ces that fin-al-ly pronounced the words just did escape from vocal cords as taut as bailing wire. And the words they managed to read, pronouncing them properly, were astounding. Because Italian is written as it is pronounced, I imagined compositions of precocious brilliance. Little Carmela was looking at me with her large, sad brown eyes. She had finished, and I seemed not to approve. I told her how well she had read, how clever she was and asked how she had learned so fast. She stuck her head down in my lap, then looked up and giggled happily.

"Tell me, Carmela, what is the story about? You must know the rest of it too."

Her look of complete mystification told me the answer, that was reinforced as, one by one, the other children read. They could pronounce the words. Nothing had been said about any meaning the words might have. And so another step toward learning by rote had been masterfully accomplished.

I should not have been surprised. I had spent the

evening before with a peasant family I have known for fifteen years. One of their sons, Salvatore, had just finished his military service and was looking for a job. When I first remember him, he was perhaps nine, a small sturdy boy with delicate features, gray eyes and dry blond hair, like a new broom, that stuck up and out from an amazing number of cowlicks. He was shy, and I think, people puzzled him, for he never looked directly at them except to decide whether they were serious or teasing. Then, as though their faces held the answers to all mysteries, he would stare at them. He did not talk a lot either. Once he took me for a walk along the boundaries of his father's fields, which he knew followed a line sighted from the top of the hill, down between two oak trees, along a bean field as far as the copse where a fox lived, and from below the well to that stretch off to the right where the third branch of one particular fig tree points. He also showed me the trap he had built to catch the fox, who was eating their chickens. So far it had not worked. He had made himself a slingshot in case the fox showed himself in daylight. He never did. Before I left he fed the chickens and explained the economic advantages of raising pigeons. His mother teased him for being so willing at home and such a mule at school.

He shrugged. "I want to be outside," was all he said.

Perhaps two years later he volunteered to show me a brigands' cave, which turned out to be a black slit under a large rock ledge. He instructed me in just how to crawl through the narrow passage so that he could prove to me there was a big room behind where the brigands hid, that is what the shepherds had said. I did as I was told and found enough sheep droppings to prove, at least, that the shepherds and their flocks had escaped from the winter winds. He told me the band kept its guns there, and I nodded solemnly.

As he grew older he still liked to be outside, to work with his father, and school was still a punishment for him. He was not stupid; no one had ever managed to connect school subjects with the world that interested him. He repeated the fifth grade and went reluctantly into the middle school, where he stumbled again in the seventh grade, but did take and pass the final examination. He had his piece of paper.

He was sixteen then. The delicate features had coarsened and his voice had become a rasping basso profondo. Only his hair reminded me of the nine-year-old boy with the slingshot and the brigands' cave. He worked all summer for his father. In the fall he repaired shovels and picks, cut wood and then there were no more chores. His father said he could not sit out the winter, so he did what his friends had done: he went to Germany. The night before he left, he came to call on me, wearing a new white shirt with a collar so starched it seemed the points would perforate the cloth, and a pair of tight beige wool trousers, also new, already too tight for him and too cheap to last a month. This was his finery for the trip. On his feet he still wore the dung-caked farm boots of other years. He muttered over and over again,

"I'll get along. Don't know what I'm going to do exactly, but I'll get along. Don't worry."

He did for four years, carrying stones on a construction job. When he was called up for military service, he left Germany and put in his fifteen months without complaint. The night I met him again he was one of six hundred young men twenty-one years old to be examined for nine jobs in a factory some fifty kilometers away in the valley. Someone in the family had wheedled a recommendation from a local man, supposed to be influential, who had also obligingly provided a list of probable questions. When I arrived Salvatore was sitting in front of the fire puzzling over the questions. Syllable by syllable he muttered the words to himself, then shook his head and started again. He was reading as little Carmela did the next evening. The sounds were right, but they meant nothing to him. He was twenty-one, she, six. Trying to make a joke of it, I offered to be the Grand Inquisitor and read the questions to him.

"What form of government does Italy have? Italy is a . . ." (Republic)

"It's in Rome. Those people in Rome . . ." He went no further.

"Who is the President of Italy?" (This was sixty days after the last presidential election: Leone.)

"How should I know? DeGasperi. Wasn't he the famous one?"

"How is the President elected?" (By Parliament with a two-thirds majority of the voting members.)

"I guess in the elections. Next May we have elections."

"Who is the President of the United States?"

"Nixon."

"Who is the Pope and what is he?" (Pope Paul.)

"It's Pope John. He's the Bishop's boss."

"Where does he live?" (The Vatican.)

"Rome."

"No, they don't mean just Rome. More specific than that. Where?" He did not know.

We ran aground forever on "What are your social

responsibilities?" They had become fashionable since he left school: the concept meant nothing to him. His younger sister found a textbook of hers with a single paragraph defining social responsibilities and told him to memorize it. He went off into the bedroom for twenty minutes. When he joined us again, he was sweating and red-faced.

"I can't memorize that. I don't understand the words."

Nor could he write the answers to the other questions in anything resembling Italian. He is not stupid, but after ten years in school, four years in Germany and fifteen months of military service, he is a functional illiterate. When I asked him if he had changed his mind about farming, he said,

"No, but you know how it is. Mamma's right. Everyone makes fun of peasants. I thought if I could get this job, maybe it would be better. I wouldn't just be a peasant."

I do not think Carmela and her little friends will be any more at ease with the mechanics of reading and writing than Salvatore, but I cannot feel that it is entirely their fault. Nor can their mothers do a great deal to help them. They know the teachers pay perfunctory attention to their classes. They see their children running errands and they hear the teacher screaming in dialect, but when they ask how they can help their children, they are told they are illiterate and can do nothing. They must wait until the end of the year to see if their children pass or fail. And at the end of five years those same illiterate mothers know their children do not write properly, still speak dialect, and read only comic books with ease. They have that first piece of paper. If they are sent on to finish the *scuola dell'obbligo*, the three years of the lower middle school with French and English and worst of all more Italian, they may have another piece of paper, but the question cannot be avoided — will they know how to do anything? Will they speak enough Italian to get around Rome or Milan where they must go to find work? Will they be able to answer the questions on Salvatore's quiz? Will they get jobs? Apparently not. Each spring I find more young girls hoeing beans with their mothers, and when I ask if they have finished school, whether the girl nods yes or no, the mother always adds:

"But what's the difference? The choice is still the same. She can sit up there and learn to embroider, while she waits to find a husband, or she can come down here and learn to work — and make some money besides."

And the boys go to Germany.

Several days after my misadventures with reading and writing I ran into a young teacher I know. Years ago we saw each other every day or so in the way normal to village life, and since then we have met four or five times a year, sometimes casually at shops or in the market, sometimes at formal meetings and at other times when, for no particular reason, we have talked alone at length. I know odd things about her that I would not know, would not expect to know, in a different sort of community.

Pinuccia was next to the youngest child in a family of three sons and four daughters. Her father was a tailor. He died ten years ago, shortly after ready-made clothes became available in the weekly market, but his trade had never produced a living in a town where old suits are more often turned than new ones ordered. Every morning of his life he peddled slowly down the Corso on his bicycle and just as slowly out to a few acres of land he owned. He plowed, hoed, planted or picked as the season dictated and then in the late afternoon pushed the bicycle, now piled high with bundles of firewood, slowly back to town and up the Corso. It was the land that fed the family, but his wife and children always maintained that he was a professional man whose hobby was farming and arranged the façade of their lives accordingly.

Signora Di Santis, Pinuccia's mother, is considered very devout. Each morning with her black lace veil firmly twisted under her chin, she settles into a particular seat on a particular aisle to await the beginning of Mass. She is always early, but something about her stiff, disapproving back suggests everyone else, even the priest, is late. She repeats the performance in the evening for Rosary. She is so regular that children ask their mothers very seriously if the church is Signora Di Santis' house. Between functions she is at home, invisible, cooking one assumes, mending probably, and though she thinks it is a secret, she used to spend that time making the trousers of the occasional suit commissioned from her husband. It is not strange that her nickname should be *La Pantalonaia* — the pants-maker — nor that her husband's nickname was Bartoli, after Gino Bartoli, one of the great Italian bicycle racers.

Their ambition was to raise seven *"Professori,"* but financial pressures and nature, most especially nature, worked against them. Of the sons one is a bookkeeper, one a driver for the government insurance agency and one is unemployed, but has stood for every civil service examination posted in the last eight years and so is said to be "waiting." Of the girls, one is a nursery teacher, unemployed, two went to Normal School, Pinuccia being the one who managed to *win* a place as a permanent elementary teacher, and the fourth and youngest did not make it through the upper middle school and remains in her early thirties *una signorina da maritare*, a young lady to be married, which is more tactful than saying bluntly that she is a spinster. She is very much under her mother's command. The other six have married, not as well as they should, according to their mother, who now enjoys the luxury of a small pension paid in Money and the services of two full-time attendants — her youngest daughter and her daughter-in-law, the one married to the "waiting" son. He has been allowed to take up farming as a hobby.

Twelve years ago, when she first started teaching, Pinuccia was a small-boned, solid young woman with a broad face, not really round, high cheekbones and large brown eyes, so dark they conceal her most fleeting interest. She turns them full on anyone who talks to her, but they never betray what she sees, much less what she thinks. Bright red cheeks were her one natural asset, which, probably believing high color to be a sign of low birth, she disguised with sallow, opaque makeup. In her enthusiasm she sometimes applied it so heavily that, when it dried, brownish lines checked it like china exposed too long to heat. She was always neatly and simply dressed except for *feste* when she could be astonishing in tight violet satin a-swirl with rainbow peonies. Her one external defect, not that she has ever considered it such, is a hoarse, rough voice, which time and the strains of marriage have made raucous.

The local euphemisms of refined speech bellowed out by Pinuccia sound like jokes, but she is serious when she calls feet "extremities" or excuses the term "pork" when discussing meat. She would never get in the front seat of a car without saying to the passengers in back, "*Scusate le spalle*" — "Excuse the shoulders," i.e., my turning my back — and she is always coyly *in stato interessante,* never pregnant. From the young woman who used to say, "In the city they do such and such," knowingly and then add, "Don't they?" in a quiet plea for information, she has become an imitation of what she thought she wanted to be. At times she does not convince herself, but her inferiors will never be allowed to guess it.

She married a clerk in the tax office ten years older than she and balding. He is almost a parody so much does he look what he is in his sturdy, formless suit and his shoes with the heavy rubber soles. An inspection of his hands will show deepset splodges of ink and a long, not very clean nail on the little finger. He used to drift around town aimlessly in the afternoon and evening, neither gentry nor peasant. Now he has a battered Fiat 600 and a little tweed hat and he *drives* aimlessly around town. It is not out of character that he is a vicious gossip. They have had three children in five years, but no matter how many more may come, Pinuccia will never resign her job any more than she will ever approve of birth control or divorce.

Pinuccia is an authority on her "rights" and always arranges for her full quota of maternity leave and the daily time off allowed for nursing her new baby. She also talks a great deal about the more or less intimate arrangements of her household. So it is that I know her husband wears undershirts she knits for him, which he changes once every two weeks when he bathes (if it is not too cold). She still uses washable sanitary towels and does not touch water on "those days." Her husband loves *baccalà* (dried cod), insists on unrefined olive oil and drinks a liter of wine with lunch. One of her children suffers from liver trouble. She swaddles her babies for at least the first six months and feels that as long as she is nursing, she is safe from pregnancy.

Much of her physical neatness has disappeared. Blouses are apt to be spotted; buttons are often missing. Her hair is only washed for holidays and her figure bulges with strange lumps and protuberances. Everything about her has sagged into lethargy except her tongue. Recently she told me that her mother-in-law had moved into their two bedroom flat with them. When I asked how it was working out, she did not understand why her answer amused me.

"Well, she's a help in the house, of course, but she's always telling my husband what to do and that makes me mad. My mother is right — one family, one house. You can't put two feet in one shoe."

She is neither better nor worse than the others. She does her work well, as she understands it, but, if she were to tell the truth, it is a source of income and social standing, not a vocation. This is the conversation I had with her about Salvatore and the children who had read to me. Clearly if there is to be change, she will not initiate it.

"Of course I teach because I love my work, but if you only knew how impossible it is with *these* children. They come to school dirty, half asleep with their homework not done, and they're pigheaded as well. If I ask them why they didn't do their work, they just shrug. They don't care. They don't see any point in going to school.

You can't expect any help from their families either. They're all illiterate, or almost all. I have three or four children out of thirty who are bright — *oh Dio*, not brilliant, but what you might call teachable — who try to speak well and they write well too, but, of course, their families are different. One's the daughter of another teacher, one's the son of a doctor, another the son of a colleague of my husband's. The rest of them — well — I do my best, but you end up screaming at them, and I admit it — in dialect. They're too thick to understand Italian, or they pretend to be. By the end of the morning I'm exhausted. It's hard to teach and look after a house and a family too. That's why I ask for the morning turn. Then by the time my husband comes home at two, everything's ready for lunch and the day can go on normally. But it's hard work.

"Sometimes they insist we go to courses. Then my husband doesn't like it. They're usually a waste of time too. *Scuola Attiva, Scuola Democratica*, all those social workers running around, finding out if children are healthy and wanting us to find out. I say that's up to doctors and for the rest, school-this or school-that may be fashionable for a time, but they pass, and we're still left teaching them to read and write.

"They've just put nursery schools under public instruction and everything's still disorganized, but in a few years, as I see it, children will learn their letters at nursery and the elementary schoolteacher's work will be easier — that is if the Ministry in Rome doesn't change the program. They change things, sometimes just to change them. I mean from a way that worked to one that just shouldn't be — like — for instance — having mixed classes — boys and girls together, using the same texts too. Now that may be all right in Anglo-Saxon countries. We always copy them as though their ideas and ways of doing things were better than ours. I don't like all this foreign influence — present company excluded, of course. *He* wasn't wrong when *he* said Italy for the Italians! As I say, mixed classes may be all right in Anglo-Saxon countries, but not in Italy. There's nothing you can do about it — we're hot-blooded. You put children together and they're just like animals, leaving out how these live at home. They start playing nasty games and then where does it stop? That's what they don't realize in Rome. Hot blood, I tell you. Hot blood! Boys and girls should not be mixed in classes together.

"And the textbooks. It's the same thing. I'm teaching them what is right, no? That's the job of a teacher, no? What a boy needs to know is different from what a girl needs. They have to know what's expected of them. I always used such a good book with the girls — I can't now, but before, yes — about the Madonna being a mother, just like our own and someday we too will be mothers, so we must respect ours, help them take care of the house and the babies. It wasn't a sermon, but it was right for these girls. After all, why do they need to read and write? They don't really, except — yes, agreed, everyone should know *how* — but what they need to know is how they are supposed to act. If we don't tell them, who will?

"No, I don't feel I should be preparing the girls for work in a factory or any other career — not even the boys. These are peasant children. Their minds aren't refined like city children's. Peasants are not civilized people, and making them restless for something they can't have, couldn't do if they had the chance — why — it would be silly. All right, the world is changing, but not that much and not down here. Listen to me, I know these people. The children need to know what is Right and Wrong without blowing up their heads with ideas they can never understand, and if you don't agree, I'm sorry, but *we* know what they need."

"We never did find one of the copper boilers. My little boy left the old house carrying it, but he doesn't remember where he stopped along the way. All I know is he went down into the valley and up, and we had to take the long way around with the furniture. It was bad enough hauling the heavy things without making the climb. A truck? After we bought light fixtures and a stove — with the fireplace and a gas burner, we'd never needed a stove before — there wasn't any money left. Besides, the truck couldn't get to our old house, so everything had to be carried as far as the Piazza anyway. My sisters and my mother helped. It took all day, but we finished before dark. We don't have enough furniture, and what we have is old and beaten up, but I don't care — just to have two bedrooms and a toilet with water, sometimes. That's enough for now.

"If I buy two piglets maybe by Christmas I can begin to think about a real bed for the children, that is, if my husband doesn't take the money. The only reason he agreed to move was the rent. It's a thousand lire ($1.50) a month cheaper. In his mind he's already spent it more times than there are months left in his life. He didn't want to come over here to the new houses. He says we're too far from the Piazza, there aren't any stores. We're second class citizens, he says, with no postman, no garbage collection, no protection. But men always talk about

unimportant things. We never get any mail
and there'll be garbage collection — someday.
As for the Piazza, he can walk there, just
like me. Men are like that, always holding out
for the unimportant things. They don't spend
much time in a house, and all they really
want is their pasta ready when they come in.
Beyond that, separate bedrooms, toilets,
water in the house, they don't care. If they
don't have them, they talk about them, mind
you, but we care. We have to. We're the
ones who have to make do — however it is."

Cettina

Peppina, Ninetta and Teresa are not totally self-sacrificing. When they struggle for their families, they struggle for their own survival as well. They do not conceive of their lives as separate from their families', nor are they driven to find ideal situations for themselves. They succeed if they manage the situations in which they find themselves. Cettina, who is almost a generation younger, has chosen the opposite tack, leaving her husband and two children to wallow and bounce in her wake like captive dinghies. She may be more typical than one would like to think.

She and her friends grew up with one eye firmly fixed at the television keyhole. They watched everyone's favorite program, thirty minutes of back-to-back commercials, and became avid consumers, if only in their minds. All they need do was wait for the "Italian Miracle" to overcome them, like some golden contagious disease. They wiled away their time with variety shows, give-away programs and old American films. Their knowledge of movie stars' lives and the trousseau of the Shah of

Iran's new bride was encyclopedic; they never missed an issue of a magazine revealingly called *Grand Hotel.* They brushed aside the grumbling pessimism of their parents with brutal scorn that would have earned their mothers a beating. "What do *you* know about the world? You're buried in this place even God has forgotten. Work, work, work! That's all you know! And what did you get for it? Nothing! Well, it's different now. *We're* not dumb, like you." They were too busy honing their dreams and pretensions to worry about school. They were casual about their examinations and even more casual about their failures. They were the greedy voyeurs of Real Life, and when it remained an elusive coming attraction, they still imagined themselves, if not with the white telephone, at least with a white rug on the floor and a husband to match.

Fifteen, even ten years ago it was hard to guess what Cettina's life would actually be. At first her mother, Maria, ignored those strange rumblings of change, dismissing them as the curious events and tastes of that other world. She did not expect to buy "Moplan plastic," anymore than she expected to join the Russians junketing in space, or the Chinese colonizing Albania. Let the Madonna of Lourdes peregrinate in a helicopter and Alberto Sordi extol the pleasures of those most improbable mechanisms, the washing machine and the dishwasher. Interesting to look at, but hardly relevant when you and four children have just moved from a one-room house over a stall to a three-room apartment that seldom has water and enough electricity to play the radio only if the lights are turned off. And sanitary rags soak adequately enough in the old enamel basin. To Maria life was an entirely practical matter. She had no intention of wasting money on newfangled things for no better reason than they were newfangled. That television set was a good example.

"Now why in God's name did we need *that* when some nights you can't get a glimmer out of it? Besides, it brings the whole neighborhood tracking into my front room and keeps two of the children from going to sleep on the cot. Some nights, when the show's over and I turn on the lights, everybody's asleep — men, women and children — all asleep! So why did we need it? They can sleep at home." When she was irritated, which was often, her voice was a shrill tattoo. "Well, the answer is my husband said he wasn't going to be taken for someone dying of hunger, especially not now when he *almost* has a job. So — if you don't count the cafés — we have the first set in town, and I hope everybody's impressed because those time-notes are going to rest heavy on my stomach for thirty-six months."

Whatever dreams and longings may have assailed Maria's youth had long since been corroded by fact. She admits that she had thought, had tried, had sort of set one target for herself: she did not want to marry a peasant. Her looks had been her only capital. As a girl she was tall and slender with fine, even features and deep blue eyes that twinkled as though everything she saw amused her. She had more than her share of admirers, all smaller than she, but what difference did that make? Short men like big women, she would say and laugh. Makes them feel big and masculine. When she was twelve, she started working in the fields, at first with her family to learn and then as a day laborer. She was in demand, not entirely for her youth and strength, but as often as she changed *padroni*, she met only peasant boys.

Then one winter in town a young man named Pancrazio came evenings to sit by the fire. His father had been a peasant and had died young, and his widowed mother owned nothing except her one-room house with the stall below. She had raised a daughter and a son on what she earned as a servant in the house of her husband's *padrone* and the rent from the stall, when, indeed, she found someone who needed it. Eventually she sold it to raise a dowry for her daughter. Pancrazio had not approved. Not only was he being cheated of his share, but so close to the Piazza, the stall would be highly valuable as a garage — someday — when the town could boast more than two cars, both for hire, that stood night and day by the fountain. Though it could house only two, or at the most, three Topolinos, Pancrazio had imagined himself running an establishment for the town gentry. He had recognized early that neither the land nor manual labor offered a future with respect. A living, yes, but not respect. He was an observant young man and had ample time to watch and speculate about the mores of his betters. He has done his best to copy what he understood as the essence of their superiority. His little fingernails are long horny talons. If his children have, at times, gone to bed hungry, he has always worn worsted trousers, a jacket, a shirt with some remnant of a collar and a striped, rather greasy tie which, when it is not serving as his badge of respectability, hangs, still tied and ready for an emergency, on the inside knob of his front door. Before he saved enough money to buy a secondhand overcoat, I have seen him in midwinter with only a wool scarf added to his usual finery, standing, shivering in the Piazza. His father's black wheel cape hangs on a nail in his front hall, but he would have frozen rather than throw it around his shoulders and be labeled a peasant. When the change in his pocket was still a handout his mother could ill afford, he smoked expensive cigarettes and offered coffee to anyone standing at the counter as he drank his own, an expansive gesture that men, not rich but more prosperous than he, learned to take advantage of with only the slightest nod of thanks.

The years have passed bringing some security, if not prosperity, to Pancrazio, who is as dogged as ever in his pursuit of the appearance of gentility. Now he drinks French cognac between the hands of his afternoon card games and drives to the Piazza in an ancient Fiat 500 whose seizures of mechanical *grand mal* strew the road with bolts, washers and assorted bits of anonymous metal and threaten to disembowel it before Pancrazio can pay the final installment. Until recently Maria worked in the fields whenever her health and abortions and the births that have produced six children allowed. He made her stop, though they still needed the money, because it did not "look right."

At no time can Pancrazio have been a romantic figure. He is not tall and his body, like a laboratory skeleton, is all elbows, shoulder blades and knees. As Maria sees him, he is not just thin, but "fine-boned," which, since it is not a peasant quality, is to be admired. He has the wizened, young-old face of the half-starved child with wide, bulging eyes, a pinched mouth and a long thin nose. In compensation for his meager physical charms he did not want to be a peasant and he owned his own house, or would when his mother died. If the first was enough for Maria, the second convinced her family. They were soon married and installed in that one room with his mother. There they stayed for twelve years, and there four of their children were born.

Pancrazio had no regular work. He delivered tele-

grams and special delivery letters for the post office at ten
lire (1.6 cents) each. If there were ten in one day, an
unlikely flood, something very important had happened
in town. He would take around wedding invitations and
baptismal announcements for the same price, underbid-
ding the government by ten *lire*. No errand was beneath
him. If enough people needed certificates or forms filed,
he took the six A.M. bus to the provincial seat and returned at four P.M. for a flat charge of 300 *lire* (48
cents) per person. He bought detergent, a new and expensive miracle of the moment, in bulk, packaged it in
five kilo bags (minus a hundred grams or so that he
considered his legitimate commission) and sold them at a
price which was cheap from the consumer's point of
view, highly profitable from his. There was a period
when he went regularly to Naples to return with a duffle
bag full of the pocket radios that were so popular.
Usually he had a few cartons of smuggled American cigarettes and for a while he considered trafficking in television sets, but was discouraged by their unwieldy size and
the increased danger involved. He also developed a quiet
sideline; he supplied women willing to oblige the government clerks who lived out their dreary weeks in
rented rooms, waiting to go home for Saturday night and
Sunday.

"Professional activities" and natural inclination
kept him in the Piazza. In a sense his living depended on
his availability and his knowledge of everything that had
happened or was likely to happen. He had several
sources of information, but the *Comune* was undoubtedly the best. The central hall was a general waiting
room which originally attracted him because it was dry
and warm in winter, cool in summer. For several months

he sat with all the others, as though waiting, but ready to ease his way out onto the stairs at the first sight of the Secretary or the Mayor. Then, timidly at first, he helped people fill out forms (incidentally acquiring further business for his trips to the provincial seat): no one objected. A little table was even brought from one of the offices and put down for him just inside the door. He began to keep regular hours. Soon the clerks counted on him to bring in their midmorning coffee and entrusted him with the answering of their telephones if they wanted to skip out to the Piazza on a private errand.

His unofficial permanence was well-established, when the Secretary was transferred. His replacement, who had worked as a clerk in larger townships, had just qualified for promotion, and like most newly annointed potentates, he was more engaged with his perquisites than his duties. The first day, as he left the town hall precisely at one, an hour before the official closing, he handed Pancrazio a stack of envelopes, wished him "good appetite," and walked away toward the Piazza. As Pancrazio tells the story, he is not a man to refuse a favor to someone as important as the town Secretary, but the next day the scene was repeated with no comment beyond "good appetite." And the next and the next. The fifth day Pancrazio was absent from his little desk in the hall. On the sixth, just before nine o'clock, the Secretary called him into his office, dressed him down for his negligence of the day before and then dismissed him, handing over a packet of accounts which were, he said, needed immediately by the town paymaster. Pancrazio might be willing to do a favor, but he would not be *ordered* to do anything for which he was not paid — and he said so.

"Insubordination," the Secretary snorted. "I'll not

tolerate insubordination from an employee. Now get out!"

"You can't insult me that way," Pancrazio shouted.

Each man was so protective of his own dignity that he failed to recognize the misunderstanding until two clerks from the Registry Office rushed in to arbitrate. They guaranteed that Pancrazio was not a government employee who had declared an independent strike for higher wages, and they assured him that the Secretary thought he was legally employed and therefore negligent in the performance of his duties. Pancrazio was deeply offended. His very honor had been questioned: nothing short of a public apology could undo the harm to his reputation. The Secretary called for silence. He needed to think, he said. Finally he turned, riffled through some files until he found several pages of figures clipped together and settled down to study them, ticking off items with his pen. In the years that followed we all learned that he suspected the Ministry of the Interior of a campaign, a systematic campaign, to demean him. He measured power by the number of minions who served it and in this instance he had a *right* to a messenger, as well as an "usher": that he had neither was a calculated insult. Pancrazio has never understood why or how, but when he left the Secretary's office that morning it was as the new, "provisional" town messenger with a salary of $16 a month, lifted from a relief fund for flood victims, and poacher's rights on all suppliants to the *Comune*.

He held this *quasi* post until six years ago when the *Comune* was judged worthy of an "usher" — a general factotum, janitor and monitor of the waiting room — who was to be chosen from among crippled war veterans, orphans or civilian casualties. Pancrazio was technically ineligible and at the same time the strongest contender, a situation so normal in local affairs that no one noticed any contradiction. Officially Rome might establish the *modus operandi*, but in practice the town council used more pragmatic methods. The most fleeting consideration of the secrets Pancrazio knew confirmed his desirability. His veiled hints elicited veiled suggestions. In the Piazza he talked of his years of loyal, self-sacrificing service and of the promise made to him by the Secretary who hired him, a promise, he implied, which amounted to automatic tenure, albeit an *in pectore* appointment. Behind the scenes he worked with "friendly colleagues," as he called them, to fabricate an impressive collection of certificates, all of them false: one verified his poverty, one that he lived in housing condemned as unsafe and insanitary, and the last and most important stated him to be "somewhat" disabled by scars on his lungs believed to be the result of acute TB, now inactive, but contracted *during* the war. So by bureaucratic grace and omniscient hindsight Pancrazio became an impoverished civilian casualty of a war that had in no way touched him and *ipso facto* a municipal employee with a minimal but sure salary, government health insurance and a pension.

Strangely his new status brought few changes. He did give up his lucrative procuring activities (except for a few prominent and discreet clients he could not deny) as unbecoming a man of his position, and he did pay a deposit on the dimpled Fiat, which he did not need, could not afford, but which was again a matter of his position. Evenings had never been spent at home. Now, instead of standing in the Piazza, he and his "colleagues" took over the back room of a wine shop where they played cards, ate meat they had cooked by the owner's wife, and of course drank liters of inky red wine. When he came home, he was surly and half drunk. The children soon learned to be asleep.

For Maria little or nothing had changed. Work and worry, six children and more than a little dissatisfaction had taken their toll. It had not escaped her that somehow her plan had gone awry, that she was not married to a peasant, but had remained one herself and so must accept the toil and low esteem of her lot. She was still an imposing figure, tall and rather stout with the usual prolapsed and so protruding uterus. While her body thickened, her face, quite improbably, shriveled, leaving an all-over tracery of fine lines, and the loss of most of her teeth allowed her lips and the flesh around them to sink inward until she looked like one of those old women who refuse to wear dentures. She was forty-five. She suffered from frequent liver, which we would call gallbladder, attacks, and if she carried heavy weights any distance, was inclined to hemorrhage, but she still worked in the fields when she could and did the housework and cooking for a teacher. She worked from necessity, not choice. Pancrazio has always been less than generous with household money, considering bread and pasta sufficient food and any covering that was modest, clothing for his family. On market days Maria was a regular and ingenious customer at the secondhand stall and in the kitchen performed miracles with baked *timballo* and *lasagna,* but unless she worked there was not enough money to feed and clothe the children. Much of the daily responsibility for them fell to Cettina, who, as the eldest girl, was expected to be her mother's deputy.

At ten Cettina was a short, small-boned little girl with long dark hair, sloe eyes and a nose that appeared to have grown faster than the rest of her. Its length added a peculiar quality of age and wisdom to her face, which a peremptory manner only confirmed. It was always hard to remember she was a child. She enjoyed her power over her brothers and sisters more than the nuisance of caring for them, and thought that if she locked them in the house, they were safe and she, free to go visiting.

Time and again Maria warned her not to leave them and then, guided by nothing more reasonable than intuition, reappeared unexpectedly to make sure they had not been abandoned to their destructive amusements. (She was right to worry. Once little Bruno set fire to a curtain with the candles he had lighted on his "pretend" altar. His devotion to realism kept him from being hurt. When the fire started, he was in the kitchen, searching through the cupboard for bread that could be his Host.) Three times she discovered them locked in and three times she searched for Cettina and licked her where she found her, in front of everyone who was there. Her apology was always the same: "You can't reason with her, but you *can* shame her." It did seem that no other punishment made any impression on her. Once when she was perhaps fourteen, I heard her mother tell her to be home by dark.

"I won't," she said. "No one else has to be home that early. Just make me, if you can."

"Try me, if you dare," was Maria's answer. Cettina did. When it was completely dark and there was no longer any hope, Maria went out and marched along the road until she found her in front of a shop, giggling with friends.

"Eyeeh, so there you are. It's dark, or hadn't you

noticed?" she added with heavy sarcasm. "You come home when I tell you, or you get out of my house. I won't have any *puttane!* Now move!" and she cuffed her on one ear. Cettina stood, half-stunned, looking at her mother. When she cuffed her on the other ear, Cettina started running. Maria was right behind her, slapping her head and kicking her legs whenever she could reach them. After that Cettina could always be seen at twilight, trudging, head down toward home. The same scene was repeated over mini-skirts and then slacks; both battles Maria ultimately lost to general acceptance, but not before she had beaten Cettina in front of her friends and accused her of being immodest, immoral and a waster of money. She heard in reply that "Times have changed. We don't have to do what you tell us anymore, and we don't have to stay in this hole either." But, of course, she did and no matter what new fashion or manners television revealed, she obeyed her mother.

Once Cettina had accepted that the children could not be locked in the house, she had a choice: either she stayed at home, or they went with her on the curious round of visits she made every afternoon. She was not looking for friends her own age; in fact, that I remember, I never saw her play. Instead she canvassed the neighborhood until she found a group of women sewing or knitting and talking. Some were younger than her mother, some older: their age made no difference — she wanted to listen to them. At first she stood by the kitchen door, then she eased inside and leaned against the table. Her progress was slow and silent. When conversation had started up again, she slipped into a corner and squatted on her heels. She might sit there for hours listening. Undoubtedly she picked up startling — to her — bits of information, for the women, who were used to her and in

166

a way liked her (she was always willing to change a baby or run an errand) soon forgot she was in her corner. Occasionally she surprised them with a sound of wondering disbelief, like the bleat of a baby goat.

"Na-aa!" would slip out, followed by a frantic apology. "*Scusate, scusate!* I'll be quiet, really I will." And, as though to prove it, she would clamp both hands over her mouth and snicker. She knew that she could expect a warning not to tell anyone what she had heard and too, that the women would be more careful, at least for a little while.

When she had to take the brood visiting, for of the choices she preferred that, it was harder for her to be invisible. One brother she could leave playing outside, but she always had a baby in her arms, and one, two and finally three little ones to keep quiet and amused. She had a special technique. She gave each child a hunk of bread to chew on, a toy to play with and told them to keep quiet, or she would hit them. They had every reason to believe her, and if they became fractious, it was enough that she hiss "Shut up!" for them to be reminded of her threat. The babies were more pettish, but she jounced them and burped them and smothered them in kisses until they either gurgled or fell asleep. The women were accustomed to having hordes of children around and without thinking, picked them up if they fell or cried and put them in their laps. In the confusion Cettina was forgotten, and the conversations that so fascinated her continued. Exactly what she thought about them, no one knows, or even why she listened with such concentration. Watching her in later years, I have wondered if she were — even then — deciding what she would and would not accept from life.

Whenever she found me talking to her friends, curiosity overcame the reticence that was her protective coloring. She wanted to know about the United States, but her questions were statements to be confirmed or denied. Her opening gambit was always the same:

"Do you know my mother's cousin in New York?"

"What's his name, Cettina?"

"Well . . ." She would hesitate for several seconds. "Well, I guess I don't remember, but he's *very* rich. All Americans are rich, aren't they?" It was easy for her to progress from American wealth to Americans all eat out of cans? Put jelly on meat? Are divorced? Pay no attention to their parents? To their grandparents? Before she was satisfied, we were a nation of monsters, and the yes-or-no answers she required did little to redeem us. When I tried to talk to her about my country, she countered with "Do you have your machine gun here? Americans never go out without one, do they?" Her questions were childish, but her way of listening and weighing the answers was not. She considered them with neutral skepticism, as though they must match, or at least not contradict, some secret reserve of knowledge stored away in her mind.

Cettina finished the fifth grade just as the government provided southern towns with the lower middle schools whose existence had so long (slightly over thirty years — February 5, 1928) been implied by the law extending compulsory education to age fourteen. Such is the magic power of education in the South that many believed a diploma from the middle school guaranteed a job. Their later bitterness was understandable. Hope and magic were reborn with the advent of the *Liceo* and will eventually lead to the same disillusionment in the educational spiral which now produces armies of the young, educated and competent, at least in theory, for whom there are no jobs.

This was never Cettina's problem. Her academic career limped along. She repeated one year of middle school, arrived, finally, at what would be our eighth grade, failed two examinations and never tried again. At fifteen she was still a small, slender girl with the same long, shiny hair and now with hips that arched out from a reedy waist. The boys who lounged along the road every evening ogling the girls never failed to turn and admire those hips, but it was clear that were she to gain any weight, they would assume shelf-like proportions. Her face had broadened and lengthened to accommodate her nose, and if there were any imbalance it was not so much of feature as expression. She had a look of sullen sharpness, like a starving alley cat who lays in wait for some unsuspecting prey.

At fifteen she was also through with school forever, without skills and in need of a job. She refused to work in the fields. Her mother, whose original good humor had been soured by overwork and ill health, sneered, "Nobody in his right mind would hire you to work in the fields anyway." Cettina would not do housework either: "Be a maid to someone no better than me? No!"

Other possibilities were few. She apprenticed herself to a local dressmaker for pennies a day. A month later she quit because she was tired of basting. Next she was assistant cook in a local institution, but the monotony of peeling potatoes and soaking salad greens led to the discovery that she would not work without insurance. Once more she was looking for a job. Then Maria hemorrhaged again (this time after a week of loading wheat sheaves into a threshing machine), and Cettina could without loss of face say that she was needed at home to shop, cook and clean for the rest of the family.

Every day we saw her on the main road, going back and forth to town, to the market, to the bakery, to the tobacco shop. She seemed to be constantly on the road and at the most unlikely hours. She explained to everyone she met that she had forgotten to buy salt, or an egg, or a spool of thread, or that she had to deliver a package, or . . . The excuses that flowed so freely were reasonable enough, but they were offered before anyone thought to ask what she might be doing and so, suspect. The women watched her more closely and speculated. If she were looking for a particular boy, she could hardly expect to find him at 3 P.M. on a scorching August afternoon, or could she? Who would be out at all hours of the day? One of the few logical answers: a *Carabiniere*.

Under normal circumstances a girl in Southern Italy does not meet young men with whom she has not grown up, unless a brother introduces a friend, and they are very cautious in such undertakings. There are no dances, no cafés where the young can meet or even family parties that include outsiders. Whatever happens, happens on the road, between one sidelong glance and another, between jibes and jeers, exchanged by a swarm of girls and a gang of boys. The briefest exchange will be heard by at least one other girl, probably by a dozen others. Normal courtship is not a private affair: to flirt with a *Carabiniere* is immensely more complicated. They are never assigned to towns in which they have lived as civilians. Single men are billeted in police quarters and cooked for by women chosen for their total lack of physical attraction and advanced age rather than for their culinary abilities. The men are not encouraged to make friends locally, are forbidden to marry before they are twenty-six and are transferred the instant they become engaged. In a small community everything a *Carabiniere* does from his official duties to the most casual cup of coffee is public knowledge. Still, his lifetime job, his pension and the automatic, though grudging respect with which he is treated make him a good catch. Cettina had sighted her prey. She stalked him on the road, or roads might be more accurate, because her beat varied with Vittorio's assignments.

Young *Carabinieri* are as anonymous as so many plastic spoons. Everything conspires against them — the corps regulations, the uniform itself, the unstretched features of twenty-year-olds — and Vittorio was no exception. That his family moved from the South to Florence right after the war remains in my mind because it was to be so important later. Otherwise he is a shadow in a blue uniform, a boy who was quiet, rosy-cheeked and not overburdened with intelligence — all things that could be said of any *Carabiniere*. He was as defenseless as Cettina was determined in her pursuit. She had made up her mind: this was no light flirtation. She went about her maneuvers with great care, only occasionally misstepping into the no-man's-land that separates the rigid Southern concepts of propriety and wantonness. If one day she had been friendly, joking and laughing with him on the road, the next she sidled by in the shadows with her eyes lowered. One evening she would be too intent on a group of boys to notice his passing; the next, she bowed in withdrawn recognition. Vittorio was bewildered by a target that ran such an erratic course, but determined it would not get out of his sights. If he recognized her coyness as intentional, he never suspected the complexity of her other manipulations.

Cettina plotted methodically. She had no choice, for she must convince her father to acknowledge Vittorio. He would never bring him to the house — that was too much to expect — but if he met him, if he accepted, even tacitly, that the young man knew Cettina, then one difficulty had been overcome. Vittorio, who, as an outsider and especially as a *Carabiniere*, had no one to intercede for him, could later, when the time came, ask Pancrazio for a formal interview. By then her father would have found out everything there was to know about him and fully as important, Cettina would have had time to counteract any objections.

There was another complication. Her public suitor, a willowy young man with thick bushy eyebrows, large brown eyes and wavy hair, named Antonio, had to be kept dangling in the normal way to reassure him that his cause progressed. Her sidelong glances still promised a special understanding, her teasing was frankly aimed at him, rather than one of his ever-present friends. From the twinkle in his eyes it was easy to see that Antonio was deceived and happy. One of his great attractions was this open switch between his thoughts and his face. If he were told a sad story, his mouth turned down and his eyes widened with compassion. A joke started his eyebrows and the corners of his mouth dancing. Tragedy brought tears as easily as farce did peals of laughter. In many ways he was a very innocent, trusting young man. On the road Cettina might be as playful as ever, but at home she made mildly disparaging remarks about him without mentioning his name: he was dismissed as *Il Romeo disoccupato* — the unemployed Romeo. Obviously if Vittorio were to be promoted, Antonio must appear undesirable. Everything she accomplished was by indirection, which takes time and patience. Fortunately time is not money to Southerners, and patience is one of their virtues.

All of this may seem a great ado about a common dilemma of the young in love — except that Cettina was not "in love": she had found her *sistemazione* for life. She did not suffer, or pine, or yearn for Vittorio, but she did all those things for his station in life. She was trying to capture a lifetime job and would have admitted, had she been asked, that little or no emotion was involved, knowing that any woman would understand and approve. Such calculations are the assumptions of a Southern woman's life.

Her reasons for what she did may not be a credit to her, but her tenacity and skill have to be. In March Vittorio "came to the house" to make his public declaration of intent and was received with becoming reluctance, which was just further proof to him that he had chosen well. The necessary objections were put forth: her youth, the restriction which barred his marriage for several years, and his prospects — what were they? Her trousseau had to be decided upon and prepared. They were all conventional arguments required by such occasions. Eventually it was agreed that, for the moment, there would be no formal engagement. Vittorio would not be posted elsewhere and so could come to the house in the evening or walk with Cettina and her friends. Victory was hers. Several weeks later, to no one's surprise, Antonio left town and was understood to be working in San Remo — at what, no one knew.

Cettina's life changed with her new status. There

was no question now of a job or household duties; she must spend her time on her trousseau. Rather ostentatiously she carried her sewing wherever she went so that she might embroider her sheets, which appeared to run into dozens, each allocated to a particular "night." Naturally she was only doing the simpler ones herself: those for the wedding night and the two subsequent nights were entrusted to professionals. She enjoyed the fuss her friends and their mothers made over her. After all, as such things go, she had brought off quite a coup. She learned to blush becomingly, even to simper in the approved way and in general played the bride with such persistence that the wedding, instead of years off, seemed only a matter of months.

If Pancrazio enjoyed the situation almost as much as Cettina, referring to "my-future-son-in-law-the-*Carabiniere*" on the flimsiest pretexts and cataloguing the linens and their cost, Maria seemed worried. All she would say was, "There's time, there's plenty of time." She had never liked debts and they already had too many. In August Vittorio's mother invited Cettina to Florence for part of his leave. This posed a problem that Pancrazio, Maria and Cettina argued over for days: since the families had not formally agreed, should she be allowed to go? Each had his own, predictable point of view. Pancrazio was inclined to consider the invitation as outside the normal conventions and therefore, in some way that was never quite clear, an insult. Maria worried about the expense, and Cettina insisted that no matter what *they* thought, she would do as she pleased. Once it had been decided she could go, they had to agree upon a chaperone. The most appropriate person seemed to be her cousin Giovanna who was twenty and had warts, but

Pancrazio would not hear of anyone outside the immediate family. Certainly neither he nor Maria could go: Vittorio's mother and father must visit them first. The chore fell to Cettina's brother Alfredo, who was a year younger than she, but old enough to know how to behave. He was given explicit instructions for every conceivable situation and adequate money for their tickets and a few modest presents. When they returned, Alfredo was enthusiastic, but Cettina, though she insisted she had had a wonderful time, was subdued and more watchful than usual. Vittorio was as faithful as ever in his visits.

Less than a month later his mother's announcement of her immediate arrival to visit Vittorio and meet his future in-laws flushed the entire family into action. Pancrazio, insisting no one would notice the lack of an appropriate plug, borrowed an icebox and placed it conspicuously in the parlor-dining room, which, shuttered and dark, was reserved for grand occasions. At night three of the six children did sleep there, but as their presence was temporary, they were not thought of as using it. The Formica cabinets that concealed the two beds were quickly moved to a small catch-all room, a spot it seemed unlikely Vittorio's mother would penetrate, where a laundry tub was just visible behind banks of stove wood and discarded shoes. Pancrazio's mother, who was too fuddled and weak to understand anything that went on, was rooted out of bed and bundled off amid squawks and frantic strugglings to her daughter's house. On the assumption that Vittorio's mother could have a legitimate reason for seeing it, a new toilet seat was purchased. Other touches of elegance were borrowed: two hideous plastic bedside lamps with cupids and a green vase containing long red, yellow and green plastic thistles. Had there been more time other atrocities would undoubtedly have been found. Even without grandmother, a reasonable deployment of two adults and six children in two bedrooms was difficult, but no one seemed concerned about that.

The morning of the visitation Maria came panting into my house to ask me "a terrible, terrible favor." Could I, would I let her wear my dark blue flowered dress? At first I could not think which dress she meant, perhaps because I expected her to want a more elaborate one for what was, to judge by the confusion, such an overwhelming event. Instead she had chosen a simple, long-sleeved cotton of the early "sack" period. (What was a sack on me was a good deal less so on her.) While she tried it on, she babbled about food. Chicken, roast kid, special dumplings for soup, homemade pasta, sweets of all kinds: this, the food for two meals, not a series of banquets, would strain the healthiest liver. Once the question of the dress was settled, she returned to food: could she borrow two platters? That evening I found them in my kitchen, one piled high with roast meats, the other with sweets. Three days passed before Maria brought back my dress and told me what had happened.

The visit had been mercifully short. Vittorio's mother had not even wanted to sit down. What she had to say could be accomplished in the hall, she insisted, but finally relented and went into the parlor-dining room where she was also forced to accept the ritual coffee. A silent Vittorio stood beside his mother's chair, his eyes intently focused on the floor. Coffee was handed around in the oppressive silence that precedes disaster. Vittorio's mother, who was known forever after as "That One" (*Quella*), dabbed the corners of her mouth with a handkerchief — "All those prim manners of hers, like

That One could be a lady, a real lady!" — and then plunged into her prepared speech. It was a recital. She intoned her memorized phrases as she would Hail Marys. When she came to the end of a set, she gulped for breath, moved to the next bead and started her chant. She was sure they would understand her reasoning. They had sons. Every mother wanted the best for her son, especially for her son, and they would have to understand that she and Vittorio's father had not left the South, all their relatives, their home to work and slave for almost twenty years to better themselves — they owned their own house, her husband would have a pension, the children had studied, they had Careers, Real Careers, ahead of them — they had not left the South and all that was dear to them to have their son marry someone worse off than they. No mother could accept a step backward. Vittorio was young. She was sure he would find an appropriate girl, and she wished Cettina all the best, of course, but she must object to the marriage and do a mother's sad duty. As of this minute she considered the engagement as nonexistent — however — to avoid complications she had, that morning, informed Vittorio's commanding officer of her son's commitment, and he had promised to transfer him immediately. Maria mocked her: "As perhaps you do not know, that is the rule of the Corps." The tone of condescension had been almost as galling as the insult of the broken engagement. Vittorio's mother finished on that note, nor did she wait for comments or curses from Cettina's family. She stood up, collected her purse and her son and left.

Rage and shame had imposed voluntary house arrest on the entire family. Cettina sat in the parlor-dining room with the shutters once more closed; the others tiptoed up and down the hall as though someone were dead. Until she brought my dress back, Maria had not been outside the house, and she had waited until dark to do that.

"Now they say it's all my fault. That we shouldn't have let a foreigner, a stranger in the house. Besides *Carabinieri* are like that, above themselves. Tell me, what's so fancy about him? And That One! That woman! I've told Cettina that tomorrow she gets out of the house and looks for work. And never mind about Vittorio. Forget him. He's already gone anyway. *Out,* I told her, and we'll just dare people to say something about it, that's all." Five years later I heard this same woman say to a sociologist who was doing research on the background of Southern emigrants to the North, "Of course Cettina had lots of chances. There was a *Carabiniere* who wanted her, but we objected — her father and me — so it came to nothing." Like other proud and loyal mothers before her, she may believe, by now, that it happened that way. She was not the least bit disturbed by my presence.

Cettina started on another round of unsatisfactory jobs. The only one I remember was as a clerk in a notions shop. The proprietor, a very old woman, known as *"La Spagnoletta"* (one of several words for a spool of thread), had slipped into an erratic schedule geared more to her arthritis than to commerce. I always felt the sign on the door summed up her attitude: "If you *really* need something, come to the house." There was no address. Presumably everyone who should know it did. Only a vision of wealth, effortlessly acquired, could have shaken her faith in laissez-faire. In southern villages dry-cleaning was rumored to be a miraculous process, but no one actually knew because the service had never been available. There was, however, a new plant in Potenza. When ·the manager offered *La Spagnoletta* commissions if she would act as his agent, she hired Cettina to keep the shop and to accept and hand back the clothes, or as was usually the case, temporize because the plant had not yet seen fit to regurgitate them. While she sat by the shop door, waiting for trade, she could watch all the transactions, public and private, that were arranged on the town's main street. In bad weather she sat inside in the dark with a gas stove singeing her ankles. Work that is not taxing, but respectable, is hard to find. This was both. It lasted three months, until Cettina realized that *La Spagnoletta*, in dividing the deliveries, saved all those where a tip might be expected for her grandson. She quit ... again.

As long as she worked at the shop I had special pick-up and delivery service. One evening, when she had stopped on her way home to drop off two sweaters, it started to rain. She would not take my umbrella. She'had plenty of time, she said. If she were not disturbing me, she would wait. Until that evening I had never appreciated that the Italian idiom for "this and that," *il più ed il meno*, has a heavy, almost desperate quality that the English lacks. Nothing held Cettina's interest for long. She was restless and sullen. She drifted back and forth between the sitting room and the kitchen, touching pictures and flipping up the covers of books and asking questions that had no connection with anything, not even with each other. "Do you keep your shoes until they wear out?", "Why do you have so many books?", "Why is your mother wearing a hat in that picture?", "How did you learn to type?" She did not bother to listen to the

179

answers, but kept moving, touching, asking. Finally she settled down at the kitchen table and folded my sweaters.

"You should see some of the stuff we get. Not like these that keep their shape." I said she must see a lot of clothes. "Junk, most of it, or old-fashioned. Nobody here has any style. You know, someday I'm going to get out of here, and when I do, I'll throw away the rags I've got and buy all new — and I won't worry about how much they cost either. First, though, I have to get out of here . . ."

"And find a husband who can afford you," I interrupted not too kindly. She looked at me for a long time before she said anything, as though weighing how much I knew, how much she could admit.

"That's why Vittorio was a good deal," she sighed, and started arranging some straight pins on the table in triangles. "Did Ma tell you I got a letter from him? He's in Pescara now. That's what I mean. He might be stuck in a place like this for a while, but then he gets something better. He didn't say much — just that he was sorry for everything and he missed me and would I write to him. But I don't think I will." She rearranged the pins slowly. "I could get around his mother — she's a beast — but there's my father. He says why should we be insulted by some stupid *Carabiniere*'s mother? What's so fancy about them? He blames Ma because she talked him into letting Vittorio come to the house, when he knew better. No more city riffraff, he says. If I want to get married, there are plenty of boys we know all about right here." She stopped, put her head on one side and then suddenly decided to sweep up the pins. She seemed to take vicious pleasure in jabbing them, one by one, into the cushion. I wondered if she were thinking of her father or Vittorio

180

and had decided I would never know when she finished with the pins and turned on me angrily, as though I had taken sides against her.

"*You* can say, 'Marry someone here,' but look at them. Look at them! Where will they be in ten years? I'll tell you. Right here. They don't know anything else. Even if they go away, it's just to get enough to come back and eat for a while. Eating, that's as far as they can think." Her voice, always sharp, was shrill with contempt. "That's why I wanted Vittorio. Oh sure, his mother is a bitch, and toward the end I caught on that he wasn't very bright either. He could have made a little money. He didn't have to do anything wrong, just turn his head and not see, but — oh no, not him! He was too scared, except that isn't what he said. His excuse was," and she whined as she imitated him, " 'Oh, no, that wouldn't be right.' Right! *Right!* What was wrong about it? Everyone else does it; besides he didn't have to *do* anything. He was a terrible ass-kisser anyway, always after me about 'Be nice to the *Maresciallo*'s wife' and 'Remember to say good evening to the *Appuntato*' just like I was a little kid in school. So what's an *Appuntato*? He's not even an officer. Why in twenty years Vittorio could be one. 'Say good evening to the *Appuntato*.' " She made a rude noise and then turned to look out the window. "I'll go home now. It's not raining anymore, but — but — well, I didn't mean to get mad at you. It's not your fault I'm going to marry someone 'we know all about' — and who knows all about me — and spend the rest of my life, like Ma, picking dinner out of a sheep's head with roast potatoes on the side to fill me up. And I can't do anything about it, that's the worst of it." Then she repeated the phrases very slowly as though to herself. "I can't do a thing about it, that's the worst of it." And for the first time I felt sorry for her.

Antonio was back for Christmas, looking very prosperous in a checked suit and a white shirt. He had shortened his name to Toni, which was considered very big city, very chic, and his Italian had changed from the local slur, well-sprinkled with dialect, to the more precise language of the Ligurian coast. Success had brought an ebullience that the stilted demands of grammar and proper pronouns could not suffocate. He was young, happy and for the first time in his life had some money he could afford to waste. Every evening on the road he met Cettina and her friends and slowly he slipped back into the old ways of teasing. She flirted, he teased, she teased, he gave her long looks. Soon the New Year had come and he must leave again. One day when I asked how he was, Cettina told me he wrote to her occasionally. She answered if she had time.

"Toni's all right, I suppose, but I couldn't marry anyone who did *that*." Her distaste suggested he worked in a slaughterhouse or cleaned sewers: not at all, he was a waiter in a resort hotel. He had done much more than could have been expected of him, I thought, with little schooling and no training. His father was dead; his mother lived on a small pension and what she could raise on two minute fields and a vineyard that had been her dowry.

Toni was back again at Easter, and in the summer and again at Christmas, when it was finally agreed that he and Cettina would marry a year from the following summer — on one condition — that he find a job in a factory. He went to Milan, found work in a plant that produced small electric motors and an apartment with three rooms and a bath, which he shared with two cousins who had gone North with him. He was philosophical about the arrangement. He earned less than he had earned at the peak of the season, but he did not work long hours; the apartment was more comfortable than the living quarters he had been given in the hotel and not expensive because the costs were shared.

"You always have to give up some things to get others," he told me. "I don't like the work as well, but my nights are free and I have lots of friends." Once again Cettina was busy embroidering sheets and planning.

They were married in the summer of 1970 with all the pomp, confusion, bickering and tears common to such joyous occasions. Cettina wore a long white satin dress with a garland of orange blossoms crowning a surprising Empress Eugenie corkscrew hair arrangement created by a friend. Maria borrowed my flowered blue cotton again, which says something about her taste and my wardrobe. Toni's mother almost refused to come to the wedding because she could not pay her share of what she considered Cettina's extravagant arrangements for the reception. A three-piece electrified and amplified band had been hired, but could hardly have cost a great deal as the musicians were neighborhood boys, playing borrowed instruments. Finally the tears were all dried, peace was made, and we formed our little procession out on the road below Cettina's house. It was a hot, still day, and the air, thick with the acrid smell of manure and scorched hay, clung to us. By comparison the church was dank. A little boy in a black velvet suit with a white lace collar, the son of one of the witnesses, piped over and over again in his high little voice, *"Mamma, voglio fare pipi,"* and the priest chose as the subject of his homily the evils of divorce. To me the rest of the day is a blur of noise and costume changes, for the bride had requested that I wear three different dresses during the reception. I remember that the women sat together on one side of the room, the men, all in shirtsleeves, on the other and that many women danced together, in the old traditional way, two-stepping solemnly about the room, apparently undisturbed by the twanging rhythms of the rock music. When enough orange pop had been consumed and restless children had smeared melted ice cream over every available surface, and Cettina's coiffure had disintegrated into long strings, she and Toni left for some place unknown, probably Potenza.

A year passed before I saw them again. Toni brought Cettina home to have their first child. The most startling change, if their extreme "mod" clothes were accepted as the current city fashion, was a broad Milanese accent, which sounded almost real until dialect words were garbled to fit the cadence. They were as disconcerting as an American Southerner might be if he talked about chitlins, de boss, dem white folks and coon hunts in his best imitation of a Brooklynese accent. They were both very animated: Toni, even a little smug; Cettina, full of bewildering tidbits of information about the *Commissione Interna* (the internal commission, or union local), the girl at the next table's lover, a discotheque, and a shop where she bought clothes for almost nothing because, as everyone knew, they were stolen. She worked in the same factory as Toni and announced firmly that "industry is the only place the worker has any rights," a statement Toni confirmed with grave noddings of the head.

The frenetic gaiety of their stories about life in a

cosmopolitan city did not ring true to anyone who had talked to their boarders, Toni's cousins. Their extra money toward the rent had been too tempting for Cettina. She had lured them into staying with a promise to cook and launder for them. Every Friday night each contributed an equal quota to a common purse. Saturday morning Cettina shopped and Saturday afternoon they all sat down to argue. Food became the pivot of their lives. She filled the men with spaghetti; they wanted meat, vegetables and fruit. She was determined to save money. Not unnaturally Toni supported her, for neither was ravenously hungry after lunch at the factory canteen. Usually the bickering ended with Cettina's refusal to do the laundry. "I have an equal right. I work an equal day and I refuse to be your slave," she would scream against their shouts of "We damned well pay for it and we're going to get it out of your hide."

The neighbors, who tolerated noise no more willingly than they did Southerners, banged on the radiators and when that brought no results, yelled threats out the windows. Cettina answered in kind and for added measure turned the radio on full volume. Southerners dismiss ordinances that prohibit such things as noise, spitting in public places, and the disposal of garbage by a quick toss through a window, as the decorative trimmings of civilization, no more important to life than an extra touch of passementerie to a dress. Cettina was surprised by a peremptory knock at the door and stunned to find the police, investigating, courteously but firmly, a complaint of undue noise. The neighbors had acted: it was a declaration of war, repeated daily in mumbled insults on the stairs. Only one other time were they driven to such fury —when Cettina strung a wire on the outside of the building from her kitchen window to a bedroom window and hung the laundry out to drip. She ignored the first shouts that this was no Neapolitan slum, but when the woman downstairs threatened to call the police, Cettina decided she could use the drying terrace provided on the roof. Toni's cousins, who delighted in the skirmishes and reveled in her defeat, had reported her initiation in detail to their families.

Once, when she was home for a visit, she and Maria came to sit in the shade of my balcony and watch the *passeggiata*, which was the evening amusement of the gentry, the middle class and the unmarried, and the great spectator sport of the village. Now that Cettina was married, she would not parade up and down at sunset. No one could exclude her, but her presence would be a contradiction, for the promenade is fundamentally an activity of the few people with leisure and presentable clothing. That day even had Cettina wanted to, had she had the physical strength to drag herself back and forth along the road, she could not decently have done so: the baby was expected in less than a month. The two women gossiped about all that was happening, or not happening, below. Slowly twilight shrouded the hills in purple, and the cool evening breeze rippled through the plastic strips at the door, punctuating our conversation with quiet click-clicks of disapproval. Cettina talked about Milan and her life there. We listened.

She did not live in Milan at all, but out on the urban tundra, beyond the bus lines, where the sewer mains ended and satellite towns of gigantic cement shoe boxes are spawned overnight. Their apartment, the first to have been built in this nucleus, formed one side of a four-sided compound with a courtyard in the center where boys played football all day. Toni had either painted it or had it painted, she did not seem to know, but it was clean and the red and black marble chip floors received moderate praise. She loathed her neighbors singly and collectively.

"They're no better than we are, but just wait until Sunday, and you'd think they were kings and queens the way they strut around, and them nothing but common plasterers and cleaning women. They get all scrubbed up and put on their fancy clothes, and dress the baby up like a doll. Then they go out on the street and prance up and down pushing him in one of those high-wheeled baby carriages. Remember, Ma? Like the one the Queen of England had that time on television. Remember how we laughed? Well, there they go with the carriage, all snooty and full of themselves. The young ones like us, where do you suppose they go? You'd hardly think it, but they go to a film or a soccer game just the way we do. I've seen them, but of course they act like they don't know us. They're better than we are, see! Those women. They're stuck up bitches, and, and foul-mouthed — and cruel to their children too," she concluded rather foolishly. They had snubbed her and she resented it. The women did not speak to her; the men felt it their right to pinch her. I believed that, but objected mildly about the mistreatment of their children. "If you don't believe me, come up and see for yourself how they slap them around and yell at them all the time to shut up. And they put them to bed right after dinner too! If they cry, they're spanked — every baby cries. Those people just don't love their children the way we do." I might have forced myself into a discussion of the relative merits of discipline and infantile tyranny, but Maria hissed,

"Cetti! Spsst! Cetti, is that her? Down there. See her

in the red sweater?" She pointed at a shapeless woman, neither old nor young, in a black skirt, red sweater and runover, low-heeled shoes, who was hurrying along the road without a glance at the strollers. "That's the one I meant. She's on her way to the hospital right now. They say he's bad." She pointed again for Cettina, who had left her chair to crouch at the railing and peer over into the street.

"Na-aa," she said, reminding me of years before when she had sat in a corner, listening to the women talk. "How'd you know she'd be back?"

"Eh, maybe I'm old, and you say I don't know anything, but I know how people are *here*. She was bound to come back."

"Why? Come on, tell us. Why?"

"If you're so smart, you should know." Maria was enjoying herself. "Remember when she got married to Giustino? And remember that before, everyone thought she was after his brother? Well, when Carlo got hurt, I said to myself, she'll be back, never worry, she'll find a way. And she did — that's all. I thought she must be the one you'd seen up there in Milan." I was lost and said so. Cettina was glad to explain.

"I told Ma about it. I was so embarrassed. More and more people from town keep moving to where we live and it's awful. You'd think with all the other places there are, but no — Anyway, people I'd never have anything to do with here, and there they are. It's always in the market on Saturdays that they catch me and right in front of the neighbors too — 'Cettina, oyee, Cettina, wait! Don't you remember me? Wait!' I remember them all right, so I duck behind a cheese counter and wait for them to go by looking for me. That one," she pointed out

toward the road, "she was the worst, yelling and scream-
ing after me, and in those rags she wears. I was ashamed.
All my neighbors were standing right there, watching."
Slowly the conversation drifted away to other things.
Cettina talked a lot about Milan, her Milan, that is.

The factory was an hour and three buses away, but
oddly she did not complain of that. The happiest part of
her day was the time spent at work. She made friends
with the other girls in her section, many of them Southern. They taught her where to buy clothes, the latest
fashions, cheap ("Sure we knew they were stolen, but,
after all, someone's going to buy them"), how to make
up her eyes and more important, how to fool the foreman. If a girl had a complaint — persecution by a supervisor, or bad food in the canteen, or anything else — she
filed it with the local, and the management had to do
something about it.

"Remember, Ma, I told you about the supervisor —
Trevisan was his name — who always called us dirty
whores? Dirty whores, get off your rears and finish this
quota! You dirty whores do this and You dirty whores
do that until we got mad. I was so mad I told Toni about
it, but he said to forget it, that there were always cretins
wherever you go. Just pretend you don't hear him, he
said. That made me even madder, so the next day at
coffee break I talked to the girls and we figured the best
way to fix him was to file a complaint. At first we were
going to say what he called us. Then Titti, she went to
Liceo, said no, that wasn't enough and we should say he
'molested and importuned' us, like we couldn't make him
keep his hands to himself. Not that he was like that. He
wasn't. But he disappeared pretty fast — to one of the
men's sections — and good riddance, we said.

"A guy named Diego took his place. One look at Titti was enough. She's big and blond, out of a bottle, but blond. Anyway, he stood by her table all the time and talked to her and teased her. He was good-looking, but sort of la-di-da," she held up her hands and made prissy little side-to-side movements. "He'd say, 'Now remember, girls, if the foreman asks you anything, say Yes, sir, or No, sir,' and he had a thing about clean smocks, but he was all right. I warned Titti — after all he was from Puglia — but she said he was nice and always polite. He treated her like a signora, and she thought that was important. Pretty soon we saw them leave together after work. I remember Titti was always excited and sort of extra happy, and Diego stayed there by her table, laughing and talking. He was nice to the rest of us, but not like that. It didn't take much sense to figure out he had it for Titti." She sounded as scornful as usual, but there was a slight edge of envy in her voice too. "He hardly bothered to inspect what we turned out, just slipped his ticket in them and said 'Girls, work hard and do it right and we'll win a prize.' I guess Titti thought she was going to win the real prize, but instead he got her pregnant. Not that we knew then what had happened. She just sat at the table and worked and never talked to anybody or looked up. Something was wrong, but it wasn't until one night on the bus when she hinted, that I caught on. I said why didn't they just get married. That was the real trouble. He was married and had four children — four, can you imagine? — back in Puglia. Titti still had some vacation coming to her, so pretty soon she took off and got rid of the baby. While she was gone, we decided to fix Mr. Diego. It was almost too easy. We took turns not quite doing our work right and watched him slip his inspector's

190

ticket in. We worked an hour right, an hour, not quite. Took about a week before they called him over to the office: too many assemblies were getting through him that weren't right. Before Titti ever came back, he was out in the packing room. That time it worked, but still the safest way, if you want to cause someone trouble, is that complaint business. They have to do something about that, if you file."

She, and undoubtedly the others, took pride in their expertise at eliminating whatever did not suit them. It was a game that must make the lives of plant managers hell. When I asked what she would do after the baby came, I found there was another game: the legal advantages of motherhood. For the last three months she had been on "light work." The girls in her section had taught her well. She knew her "rights." She had claimed discomfort and strain from her regular work. Whether there was "light work" or not, the company was obligated to relieve her, allowing her to sit in the factory, doing nothing if necessary, for her regular pay. She had prenatal and postnatal maternity leave and then daily time off in the first six months for nursing the baby. She assured me that with careful use of her sick leave, she could stretch the time she did not work for almost a year, and even then she would not quit. She would force them to fire her in order to collect double severance pay.

"But you have nowhere to leave the baby," I objected. "Why should they pay you for almost a year when you know right now that you can't go back to work?"

"Eh, so why not?" Cettina said in her old sullen, challenging way.

"Why shouldn't she get what she can?" put in Maria. "Look at all the money the owner makes out of *her* work. Why shouldn't she get some of it back? Shouldn't all be his, anyway. She has her rights too. Besides, everybody does it. Don't they, Cettina?"

"Sure. I'd look stupid, if I didn't get as much as I can. Everybody does it."

And there it was again, the all-purpose sophism that excuses so many of our misdeeds. Recently I was reminded of our conversation that night on the balcony. There is only one large manufacturing complex in Lucania. It was built by a Northern firm that took advantage of concessions offered by the government to encourage the industrialization of the South and employs some 2700 men and 300 women. The managers of the plant have decided that, as the women marry or have children or leave for whatever reasons, they will be replaced by men. The explanation is sad but predictable. The women have been too expensive, too unsatisfactory and too troublesome to keep. They were late, sick or simply took off as it suited them. Their production level was disastrously low. They thought that once they were hired, they could do what they pleased. Now they will have to pay. Those who are left will have to work in competition with men, and there will be no more women hired. Unfortunately for them, Southern peasants are born shortsighted. They take now. Let God provide for the future. Those women who work in the plant took everything that was available and a bit more. They will not understand their elimination. It will not be a lesson, only another cause of resentment.

From all reports Cettina succeeded in her campaign to squeeze the most from maternity and then retired to lead the life of a housewife. The baby, a little boy named Damiano, suffered from colic, but naturally only at night when he could keep the entire household awake. One of Toni's cousins, who had wanted to go home for months, suddenly made up his mind, packed his bag and left. Three weeks later the other cousin lost his job as an unskilled workman on a construction crew through no misdeed or unwillingness to work. (Bad weather and tight money had brought all building to a halt, at least until spring.) He went home to spend the winter playing cards in the back room of a café.

Cettina and Toni were alone with the baby and twice as much rent to pay as the year before on half the income. She was constantly at home. Wherever she went, the baby had to go with her. She could expect nothing from her neighbors who, when they met her on the stairs, failed to see her and would not have stopped to listen to her, much less have agreed to keeping the baby. A trip to the market was a strenuous juggling act, and once there the prices terrified her. Each increase made it more unlikely that they could pay their bills at the end of the month. She saw one human being, Toni, and when she did, she fought with him. He talked about people at the factory, new people whom she did not know. He was bored sitting at home, arguing every night, so he arranged to meet friends after dinner and left Cettina with the baby. In happier times she had enjoyed those evenings. She begged to go with him. When he refused to take the baby, she accused him of waste and extravagance and cruelty and-and-and- until he slammed out of the apartment, leaving her with the only alternatives she ever really had: should she polish the furniture, clean the stove, or wax the floor no one would ever cross?

It was winter. Each day the haze was thicker, grayer and the darker shadows of the buildings that surrounded

her, more like monolithic gravestones. She was lonely
and bewildered and frightened. Nothing was as she
had imagined. She was isolated. No one knew or cared
that she was there, closed in those rooms, not even Toni.
At home they always said everyone, everything dies in
winter. Maybe they were right. In the fog she imagined
that no one would ever find her. Then there was a bliz-
zard, and she felt buried alive. Nothing was right, and it
was Toni's fault. She would fix things; she would find a
way. And she did, the classic solution: they must go
home, back to the South. Toni said somewhere in Milan
he could find extra work, a part-time job, that would ease
their tight budget. No, she complained, he would never
earn enough, and she would still be a prisoner. Well
then, they could find two more boarders, like his cousins.
That drove her to fury. He expected her to be a slave and
a slave to men she did not even know. He would leave
her alone at night, the way he did now, with strangers she
had to cook for and wash for. She was nothing but a
prisoner! Her pessimism was contagious. Toni made his
calculations, expecting failure. He convinced himself that
prices would skyrocket, that there would be a raise in
rent, which, though illegal, in practice left only two op-
tions: pay or move. He could not make enough, that was
the truth of the matter. Months of nagging and begging,
crying and ranting had undermined his determination.
He gave up and agreed to go back home.

Cettina and Toni came back two years ago. They
rent a three-room apartment in low-cost public housing.
It is as immaculate as the one they lived in outside Milan.
Cettina insisted that all the glistening kitchen equipment
be moved down, and it was, at vast expense, along with
the chairs and sofa which Toni is not allowed to touch

because the upholstery is delicate. They sit, slightly damp and unused, in the gloom of the shuttered parlor-dining room.

For ten months Toni found no work. Then finally he was hired by an oil company that had sent out a crew to repeat the soundings already made by dozens of other such crews. There is a prevailing theory that, as there is nothing else of value in Southern Italy, there must be oil. He was taken on as a simple, manual laborer, but he is bright and quick and soon he was entrusted with duties that required some skill and precision. He was cheerful again. He liked working out-of-doors and he liked his superintendent who promised to have him taken on as a permanent employee, if he agreed to travel. Toni was willing, but he had calculated without Cettina. The job was not dignified, she objected. It was all right as a fill-in, temporarily, but not permanently. He could not disgrace his family — his wife, his son, his mother. The scenes were a repetition of those in Milan, and the conclusion, the same. To save face Toni told the company that he could not travel, that his mother was ill, his wife expecting a baby. Once more he is unemployed and without prospects. He plays cards with his cousins in the same back room of the same café and if he has a coffee, he pays for it with money his mother has slipped to him. A diet of pasta has ballooned out his stomach to absurd proportions, and his eyes are hooded and listless. The last time I saw him smile was before Damiano's birth. If Cettina is around, he is monosyllabic, and it is all too easy to understand why. Any opinion or comment, no matter how harmless, is parried by Cettina with one standard, humiliating remark: "Oh keep quiet, Toni. You don't know what you're talking about." When he is at home, he watches television, but he is seldom there.

Now they have a second child, another boy, named Ludovico. Cettina likes rather high-flown names. Both children could be left with their grandmother Maria, or any one of a dozen neighbors, but Cettina says they are too delicate, she must stay with them, and so refuses all work for herself. The children are serving her well. Without them she would be unable to avoid the only work there is that she can do — another woman's shopping, cleaning and cooking. She is no more inclined now than she was ten years ago to be a maid. "Me, be a maid? Why should I?" she objects. "Why should I scrub floors for someone no better than me?" The answer is obvious. Perhaps some day, when she is hungry, it will come to her, but for now she lavishes her time on her children. Damiano is a thin, nervous child, given to fits of hysteria and sudden vomiting. Ludovico is too young to do more than sleep and eat. She is determined they will have everything she never had.

I saw her last fall at the end of one of those glittering, warm days known as the *Ottobrate*, that can be the surprise of an Italian fall. The sky was very blue, and the sun lingered, balancing on the peak of a distant stony mountain. Soon it would slip down into the dark, the wind would rise and the world would be chill again, but for the moment the town sparkled in its light, a gaudy mosaic, and the shadows were deep and soft like plum velvet. Everyone, even those few who hibernate from September to Easter, had been lured out for the evening promenade. People strolled arm in arm. Young girls, two, three, sometimes four together, swung along laughing at nothing in particular. The boys were less furtive than usual: if they wanted to, they stopped and talked to the girls. Couples who, on other evenings, paced the road in silence, their faces stiff with the leering half-smile of Etruscan grave figures, actually murmured to each other. A few even laughed at some mild, private joke. People were happier. It was that sort of evening. As I watched, I wondered how the sun spreads this golden lacquer beyond the eye to the mind and glazes the cares and boredom that blighted yesterday and will blight tomorrow. It was an idle thought that soon drifted back into that dark, silty corner of my mind where such puzzles loiter, waiting for a chance to bobble back to the surface and claim attention. This was no time to look for answers: there was too much to watch, for the *passeggiata* still fascinates me as a sort of pedestrian chess game.

The mayor passed by with his wife dragging heavily on his arm. This seems to be her way of saying, He's mine, all mine. Theirs is always a slow, almost royal progress, interrupted by bows and salutes to all the minor officials they meet and occasionally a few words granted to those of importance. To others nods are meted out in exact doses. He looked a little surprised when the Bishop did the same to him, bobbing his head courteously enough, but scowling and distracted just the same. His secretary, a thin balding young priest, always tries to compensate for his superior's gruffness with a series of nervous little inclinations which make him look an agitated puppet. No one notices. Two spinster schoolteachers of good family and advanced years came by, giggling over some tidbit of gossip. Pinuccia Di Santis nodded up at me in a self-contained way. Since our last conversation she seems unable to decide whether she disapproves of me, or I, of her. She and her husband were supporting, between them, an older woman in black, I presumed her mother-in-law, who carried a bunch of flowers and walked as though her feet hurt. They were taking advantage of a nice evening to go to the cemetery. Two aged and portly priests came next, waddling along, reading their breviaries. They looked at no one. Clearly they were out for the air and nothing else. Beyond them I noticed the Bishop rouse himself for a slow, deferential bow and a few words to a couple coming toward me. The woman was tall and slender with gray hair and gray clothes. Because he stooped, the man with her looked smaller and frail. He was bundled up in an overcoat too large for him, wore a soft felt hat, and walked slowly, jerkily, as though each step were painful. They are still a novelty to the town and are treated with exaggerated respect, partly because of his past power, partly because her haughty manner suggests they deserve it. The Judge and Her Highness, as they are known, chose to retire to his birthplace. It was not really a sentimental gesture, they simply thought it would be cheaper to live there, but the town has taken it as a great honor. They stopped to exchange a few words with the Bishop and then came slowly on toward me, both concentrating on each step they took.

By then an army of faceless pawns was milling back and forth intent on its own maneuvers, but not too intent to fail to open a wide lane for the Judge and Her Highness. In their self-absorption they almost collided with the two priests reading their breviaries, who were on their way back to town. Fortunately the *Appuntato* of *Carabinieri* was right behind them with his wife. He rushed to steady the three old gentlemen before they could come to any final harm on the ground. Then with rather ponderous dignity he brushed them off and retrieved the breviaries and hats that had skipped away in different directions. When everything was in satisfactory order, he saluted the Judge smartly, turned and saluted Her Highness with an even greater show of military precision and bowed for good measure. Her husband bobbed his head amiably, but she appeared to be totally unaware of these courtesies, or may simply have considered them her due. As though they had never been interrupted, she slipped her hand back through her husband's arm and once more they started slowly along the road. The *Appuntato* was decidedly miffed by this unceremonious dismissal. His face was hidden by the visor of his cap and the bushy moustache that is the envy of all the lower ranks, but his cheeks were flushed. He was irritated and for a moment I thought he might walk away and forget his wife. Instead he turned, offered her his arm in the exaggerated, music-hall gesture he considers gallant, and they set off again, he talking furiously to her. He could berate his wife with impunity. She is too placid to resent an undeserved scolding and too cheerful to sulk long, if she did. I thought, not for the first time, that they are a peculiarly well-matched pair, an impression which may depend entirely on their seeming to find something to say to each other always and on their physical similarity. They must both enjoy eating, for they are stout in that solid, non-flabby way that lends a certain complacence to all their movements.

Others passed and passed again, bowing or not bowing, depending on what new feuds had flashed into being and what old ones had flickered out. It all means so much when you live in such a village every day, and so little when your life is even slightly more complex. Suddenly the air was cool and damp. The sun, if not its light, had disappeared; soon the wind would come up. The Judge and Her Highness had come back and stopped to rest on the wall opposite me. They talked as they sat, he so curved that he had to cock his head sideways to see her; she, as always, looked straight ahead with that bland arrogance of the person who recognizes few things and even fewer people as worthy of her attention. I was aware of being cold, and thinking I would go inside, I glanced up the road. The *Appuntato* and his wife had turned and were strolling back toward town. After an animated conversation, they left one couple, bowed to another and another. They stopped for a word with the Director of Schools and came on slowly again, bowing and saluting. Good humor had been restored.

I stood up, this time firmly decided that I would go inside, but for good measure, or perhaps out of habit, I looked the other way and saw a most surprising vehicle rolling along toward me: an English pram. It had to be, but — With its black gondola perched high on imperious chrome springs and the spokes of its enormous wheels flashing and swirling, it is not a conveyance easy to mistake for any other in the world. Baby must feel very superior bobbling and swooping at eye level with Mummy, in the discreet privacy of that enormous shiny black hood. But here? I looked again. It *was* an English baby carriage.

The people on the road were as startled as I. They had stopped to turn and stare. A few pointed at it in disbelief; others laughed. When I first noticed it, the woman whose proud possession it was had disappeared, leaning over the wide handle, into the interior. Only a gray skirt and the tail of a dark green sweater were visible. Beside it stood a pale little boy in gray shorts and a sweater, whose hand kept reaching for and slipping off a chrome safety rail along the top of the gondola. At yet another failure he looked around to see if his mother had noticed. She had and was cross. She grabbed his arm, yanked it out full length and slapped his fingers onto the rail. Then she straightened up: it was Cettina, looking very aloof and a little pinched. She said something apparently sharp to Damiano and then pushed the carriage forward, jiggling it as she did. The springs dipped down, to erupt upward almost immediately. Poor Ludovico! Three girls passed her and, amused by the carriage, shouted after her.

"My turn next, Cettí!"

"Hey, give us a ride!"

"What is it? A new wheelbarrow?"

"That's how much you know," Cettina snarled back and gave the carriage a vicious shove that sent it lunging forward and at the same time lurching sideways in a wild shimmy. She nodded to several people who nodded and then, suddenly aware of what they had seen, turned to stare. She ignored them. Her Highness's peripheral vision must be extraordinary. Her expression never changed, but as Cettina approached the wall where they sat, she stood up and moved over in front of and facing her husband as though to protect him from danger. Cettina passed them without a glance. Her target was another; the *Appuntato* and his wife were just about even with her on the opposite side of the road. She slapped Damiano's hand back onto the rail and before she straightened up, peeked to be sure the officer and his wife were looking at her. They were. Cettina bowed slowly, regally from the waist. They continued to look at her and at the carriage with mild curiosity — and no recognition. Cettina repeated her bow just as slowly, just as regally as before. Mrs. *Appuntato* turned, said something to her husband, who smiled at her and answered, and so they passed on chatting. And I was reminded, once more, that things have never been as Cettina expected. They may never be.

"The water is not drinkable," warns the sign at the top, and yet hundreds of bottles are filled there each day and tons upon tons of clothes are washed by women who do not have water in their houses. Children come with their mothers to wait, to learn, to wring, sometimes to wash clothes under an even more incongruous graffito: "Girls make love with those who love you (love, that you may be loved)." The misspellings do honor to the benefits of compulsory schooling.

No one reads it. Few know how to read, and love is something you "make," not something you feel, so it is nonsense. The washing is more important.

L'ACQUA NON E POTABILE
A.S.
AZZ E FATE
MORE CON QELLI CHE VI AMANO
(AMATE CHE SARETE AMATE)
17-4-1968
A.S.

Epilogue

1

Optimism is beyond the Southern Italian's power to trust. He expects nothing — not from his land, from his neighbors or from his government, perhaps least of all from his governors near and far. He endures them, unable to be a partner even in organized rebellion, and so he has remained an enigma to the foreigners who have ruled him for 2,500 years. Foreigners have always invaded the South, justifying their devastation and subsequent misrule with euphemisms which are still fashionable in the conference halls of today: protection of boundaries, rather elastic ones; establishment of "just claims"; defense of the Faith (whatever) and expulsion of the usurper, preferably "The Infidel." Greed was never mentioned, but myth had it that Southern Italy was vastly rich, the true Garden of the Hesperides. So they came, and from the Greeks and Hannibal with his elephants to Napoleon, Cavour and Mussolini — the Northern Italian the most foreign of all — they conquered and were disappointed. They seized what they could find of value and then settled in to collect taxes.

In every age these disappointed foreign invaders and intrepid travelers have marveled at the past glories of Southern Italy, while deploring the character of the indigenous population and the poverty, both mental and physical, in which it is *content* to live. Their prejudices and animus and halfsights were distilled into a myth. Time has done the rest: the result, historical fact which cannot be questioned. Poverty is endemic to Southern Italy, as are erosion, aridity, dysentery, typhoid, unfinished buildings, open sewers and squalid hotels. Unfortunately all of that is true, for a variety of reasons, but hardly proves that the Southerner prefers poverty, much less the psychological profile which is its corollary. The native inhabitant is a modern paradox: he is immune to civilization. Whether or not he is the victim of some obscure genetic regressions, his character is clear to the believers of such dicta. He is a dirty, lazy, promiscuous, brutal thief (e.g., the Mafia and/or Neapolitan taxi drivers) of meager intelligence who prefers chicanery to work, eats nothing but spaghetti and garlic, sings a lot and has too many children. As a Venetian priest, exiled to Calabria for some misdemeanor, possibly lack of Christian charity, once said to me: "My parishioners are a sub-species of humanity." He was only saying out loud what every non-Southern Italian knows deep in his heart to be true.

Myths are so convenient. A sort of cerebral pabulum, they supply predigested prejudices to lazy minds and can be used to validate the status quo as the best that society can offer, *or* the exact opposite. If the shame of the innocent and the distortion of minimal truth can be discounted, myths may be harmless; their susceptibility to political manipulation is not.

Italy, as a country, invites myths, and Italians enjoy them. The Unification itself is one of the great cosmetic myths of all time. That Italians pay no taxes is another, particularly dear to Members of Parliament. It grants them unlimited franchise to levy hidden, consumer taxes to balance an official budget they have every intention of ignoring. In actual fact Italians suffer from a fiscal tapeworm that consumes perhaps as much as 20 percent of their not large incomes as they buy food (which accounts for 44 percent of annual income), contract for services and indulge in the simplest entertainment. All communications with an omnipresent government and all contracts require franked paper at just over a dollar a sheet. All receipts and all posters, even those that announce the closing of a shop for holidays, must bear a tax stamp. Italians can hardly be blamed, docile as they are, if they balk at a further direct tax on income.

But the sturdiest myth of them all is The Southern Myth. To generations of governments it was the excuse for a policy of indifference with equal taxation, softened slightly by graveside injections of emergency funds, not intended to cure the patient, but to keep him from disturbing the neighbors. Mussolini was frightened by it and chose to banish it with rhetoric. Poverty was a disgrace to the new Roman Empire. Southerners must try harder, produce more. More wheat, more children, more emigrants for the African colonies! His greatest contribution to the South may have been an enormous tax on goats which reduced the number of the beasts gnawing at what little shrubbery still held the earth to the hillsides — of course, at the expense of the local diet.

Wars, won or lost, seem to generate a period of

idealism, when people not only dream of a better world, but are willing to work for one. In the last period of postwar euphoria the Southern Myth was turned, like a worn suit, cleaned, pressed and relined to appear as The Southern Problem. Sociologists, economists, agricultural experts, social workers, teachers, doctors, architects and even politicians — in all good faith — worked together on a multilateral plan of development which was to be financed with government funds and foreign aid. No one pretended that pure altruism was at the root of such earnest, if belated frenzy. On the contrary. There were two choices: do something about the South, or accept the probability of a Communist Party victory in Italy. Political expediency may seem a cynical and immoral reason for reform, but unfortunately reform seldom appeals to legislators unless and until it is expedient and can last only so long as they receive the required, tangible results. The believer in reform is told, Produce on our terms or your money ceases. In the Italy of the 1950s this was a minor handicap: even an iniquitous system could be forced to work miracles.

I was one of those thousands of idealists who believed in and worked for the reform of the South. At last the wasteland would be reclaimed, the peasants would be released from a strangling feudal system and have their own land. Roads and schools and housing would be built. With a trained labor force, industry was possible. Anything was possible, we thought, and burrowed into our own particular projects like zealous moles. We surfaced ten or twelve years later to discover that the much-vaunted *disgregazione della società* — the breakdown of the social structure and its eventual reformation in a different pattern — which was considered inevitable and opportune by the theoreticians, had indeed taken place in the sense that it is possible to play musical chairs with a deaf cripple.

The politicians, who had always taken a myopic view of the affair, lost interest in it once they had imposed, on strict party lines, the immediate distribution of land, reclaimed or not, in districts where there was "unrest" (i.e., armed rebellion, riots, or the invasion and illegal planting of land left fallow by large owners). They underestimated the talents of the social octopus they had released, preferring to concentrate on the minutiae of their home districts. Priests were eased back into their churches and their "clientele," the mainstay of their temporal powers, taken over by the eager and concerned Member of Parliament. No question was too minor to be brought to his attention. Each public appearance reaped bushels of letters asking for a blanket, a house, a job, a pension, or war damages for the loss of a beloved hen.

The protector of one town I lived in was a Minister who even had time enough to worry over the modesty of the patients in our hospital. A road, which I know from pictures had existed for at least fifty years, passed close to the new building, on a level with the women's wards. To discourage Peeping Toms, the Minister proposed moving the road some fifty feet away, an extravagant bit of propriety that would cost between ten and twelve thousand dollars. When I suggested, as an alternative, a row of fast-growing pine trees at the edge of the road, I was dismissed as irreverent and flippant. That, however, is what was eventually done — somewhat to my amusement because by then all the cords that raised the window shutters had broken and the wards were permanently sealed off from the outside world.

With such vital matters as these under control, the

politicians were once more free to consider issues of broader importance, and there, before them, not a mirage at all, was that goose, The Southern Problem, hungry for funds. Funds. Funds were the key, and they would remain the key. And so twenty years ago the biggest bureaucratic crap game Italy has ever known began. The stakes were high, $350 billion in twenty years,* and so, to judge from the fortunes made and the sinecures obtained, were the pickings.

Meanwhile the Land Reform Agency, always something of a stepchild, had gone about its business quietly, efficiently replacing the feudal landlord with all his prerogatives and none of his spasmodic forebearance.

Another monolithic government creation, *La Cassa Per Il Mezzogiorno*, The Fund for the South, whose function it was to funnel money from various ministries into specific projects in the South (with predictable spillage along the way) had somehow proclaimed itself Czar of Highways and Public Buildings.

The game had turned out to everyone's satisfaction. Only the peasants, the supposed beneficiaries of this shuffle, felt excluded and were not yet sure how it would all end. Hundreds and hundreds of thousands of them who had not received a quota of land had been reconstituted as unskilled construction workers. They were in a bureaucratic holding pattern. Public building would more or less employ those who did not leave for the North on their own initiative, until industry, still to be invented, took up the slack. We will never know what engineering legerdemain would have supplied work for such a mass of unskilled labor. Industry was happier else-

* See *Corriere della Sera*, April 7, 1975, pg. 8, quoting statement of Minister Donat-Cattin at Christian Democratic Party Congress.

where, despite the elegant and mysteriously absorbent "infrastructures" that were provided, and public building continued in the delusion something would take its place. We have now reached the Grandeur period.

It has all happened before in other countries. Wineries were built where no grapes grew. Every town has a slaughterhouse, though it may see only one aged cow a month. Tuberculosis sanatoriums were built but never opened for lack of patients (one was finally adapted to the care of children with ringworm). Entire agricultural villages were constructed *ex nuovo* and then inaugurated by the local Minister-protector, flanked by the obligatory potted palms and unknown Powers in black suits. Still no one has ever lived in those villages. The list is sad and endless, and these, minor examples. We all had our favorites: mine — the milk pasteurization plant where the manufacturers of the machinery had to ship milk five hundred miles down the coast before they could test their installation for faults; and the entire railroad — with a full complement of stations — that was rebuilt ten years after the right-of-way had been destroyed by bombs, although it had been more conveniently replaced by a government-supported bus service. And it still goes on.

Recently (November '74) I saw a four-lane, flying highway that clings somehow for miles to a sheer rock face. When it is completed, it will cross Lucania and Puglia to Bari. Large sections are already open to traffic that would not warrant paving a two-lane dirt road. It does serve one purpose no planner imagined: it is ideal for animal fairs. And on the same trip, speaking of animals, I was taken around a vast construction being built on top of a mountain where a level area large enough to land medium-sized planes has been cleared with bulldozers. It is a *salame* factory, which will grind up 500 pigs a month. For most peasants pigs have been a family affair, each raising what he needs and can afford to keep — usually one. Now, to meet the problem of supply, several of the local well-to-do have received subsidies for the construction of feeder barns. There is a long story behind the *salame* factory. Several million dollars have already been spent to convert a group of farm buildings into an efficient, small factory: these will now be redundant. This latest incarnation with long drying sheds, scalding rooms, grinding rooms, pens and all the rest, plus a three story administration building, will cost $10 million and will give work to no more than fifty men: its owner, The Agency for Development, which is the euphonious new name of — naturally — The Land Reform Agency.

It has all happened before, but perhaps never where there was a greater chance of success. Certainly twenty-four years of manic spending have brought changes — but only a fraction of what the same expenditure *should* have accomplished. The question has to be, Could *any* country afford the waste? Now there are schools (almost none of them vocational), new housing developments in varying stages of disintegration, sewers, hospitals, and roads, roads, roads. But water is still scarce and jobs nonexistent. In the same twenty-four-year period, between four and five million people have emigrated to find work. Most are men who have left their families behind and return for visits at Christmas and Easter, sad wrenching visits. They say of themselves that they lead a *"vita sacrificata."* They are cautious men, aware that they have no training and so have no assurance of work. They are the last hired, the first given notice. Often to obtain work, they forfeit their right to insurance. They have no savings: every *lira* is sent back to care for the family they never see. These men will be the first victims of recession. Still they have only two choices: they can stay in the South and not quite starve, or they can venture to the industrial cities of the North and beyond, where they may find work, and where they know that more than ever they are considered a sub-species of humanity — or if they did not know, they soon learn.

One by one the idealists of years ago have given up and left the South. We admit to each other that it was a unique chance, but we never talk about our own private sense of inadequacy. Failure leaves a bitter aftertaste, and yet I suspect that most of us, at the first sign of real movement in the South, would believe once more that reform, real reform, was possible. Instead, the politicians keep the South like a golden whore. They have pimped for her with blatant venality. They have shamed and blackmailed respectable Italians into supporting her, lest they be accused of prejudice. They take her to every international conference and beg for help in improving her immoral existence. Then quietly they divide their share of her earnings and shove her back out on the street.

The Southern Myth is stronger than ever. Illogically it now claims that the Southerner willed the failure of the reform, and then, not content with *his* sabotage, he dared to invade the North, bringing with him the filth and crudeness of his poverty. He was offered social amnesty on the condition that he stay out of sight: he violated those terms. Now more than ever he is a despised sub-species of humanity. I have come to the conclusion that

only his own adaptability, ingenuity and hard work —
and time — can prove him otherwise.

2

Failure teaches in insidious ways. Just recently have
I realized its deadly legacy to me: a raging fear of social
myths and the tragic, shambling chaos their manipulation
can create. The day of the invader and the enlightened
traveler as inventors of myth are over. They have been
replaced by experts licensed to tinker with society, the
Social Scientists, whether anthropologists, sociologists, or
social psychologists. They germinate in the dim antiseptic
quiet of university libraries and apparently never fully
recover from certain habits acquired there: a tendency to
confuse semantic obtuseness with thought, a naive rever-
ence for methodology in itself and sometimes the humor-
less arrogance to treat the human being as a specimen
which can be reduced to decimals and diagrams. One of
their basic assumptions is that any society can be plotted,
revealing patterns of behavior. For a simple society, a
simple schema; for a complex one, a complex schema.
Once the schema exists and is accepted as valid (by the
social scientists) certain constants are established.

The isolated peasant community, as the simplest
unit in Western culture, is the natural target for such
investigations. Hardly a Mexican village survives un-
scathed. The "equipe" arrives, armed with bales of its
own in-depth questionnaire, an amazing number of
mechanical toys which will not function on the local current, cameras, a goodly supply of tinned food and its
antidote, enterovioform and finally, but perhaps most
important, firmly fixed smiles. An interpreter, who is be-

lieved to be so neutral that he would never slant or edit
what is said to him, collects a group of unemployed men,
willing to bare their souls, to reveal the intimate details
of their lives to total strangers for a token payment. Apparently the peasant is without *amour propre*, humor or
modesty. He is expected to answer the most personal,
abstruse and at times ludicrous questions with total can-
dor. (It is taken for granted that peasants are candid;
they are too unsophisticated to be anything else.) The
social scientists, trained sensitive observers, as they like
to call themselves, read the nuances of every hesitation
and smirk so adroitly, and probe so subtly, that their
preliminary conclusions are sometimes stunning, if for
no other reason, for their absolute puerility. Their disapproval of humor hampers them. It is decadent or at
best inappropriate in a serious discipline. With no apparent dissemblance it passes unrecognized in others. One
group told me the village I lived in was "remarkable":
Did I realize that an overwhelming number of the men
had stated that sexual intercourse was "practiced" (a
word favored by the observers which opened a whole
comic world of possibilities) by preference standing up?
I did; so did everyone in town. But the trained sensitive
observers never, never tumbled to the joke their questions on sexual mores had inspired in people who are not
sexual experimenters, but had decided they were being
mocked by the *professori*. Ah, the pitfalls of multiple
choice questions! Do you prefer (practice?) sexual intercourse 1) in a fully lighted room, 2) in a dimly lighted
room, 3) in a dark room? Do you prefer (practice?)
sexual intercourse 1) naked, 2) partially dressed, 3)
fully dressed? Many years ago Dr. Kinsey settled all of
that, and the Southern Italian peasant is no exception.

He is by nature and training rather prim and his crowded living conditions do nothing to ease his inhibitions.

Once all questionnaires are filled out, observations noted, quirks and anomalies documented, the "equipe" returns whence it came to consider its material. When it has been collated and correlated and sometimes culled by the arcane use of "A Principal Components Factor Analysis with Verimax Rotation," the peasant is discovered to be not only "mother-fixated," productive, non-hoarding and alcoholic (or the opposite), but he suffers from a number of mysterious afflictions which may be considered offensive in polite society: "binary oppositions," "amoral familism," and *acute* lateral mobility." It is hard to choose between such gibberish and the saccharine fantasies of perfectly honest, intelligent men, reputable sociologists, who have deluded themselves that the peasant establishes a mystical relationship with the land he tills and even further, that he takes pleasure from a life *well-lived* with little. Only Oscar Lewis and Robert Coles seem able to sidestep jargon without slipping off into sentimentality, allowing the human being his one, unique, irreducible quality — his humanity. His infinite variations — his courage, his poverty, his pettiness, his shams and his dignity — his relation to his society must be understood, not just tabulated, before common factors or constants can have any meaning.

One of the constants so well established that it is neither supposition nor respectable myth, but dogma, is that simple Western societies, peasant societies, are patrilineal and patriarchal. For twenty years I have obediently tried to convince myself that the Southern Italian towns I have lived in, worked in and studied were patriarchal in structure and for twenty years I have failed. Massive doses of sociology and social psychology, though almost fatal, have not cured me. Twenty years of thought and effort to understand Southern Italian peasants, and even more important, twenty years of listening to them and watching them are not proofs. I have no formal proofs. I know of no way to establish them: people's lives present few absolutes. My opinion was and is simply an opinion which has for too long chipped away at my resolution to ignore it.

In the end I cannot. I believe that the social structure of Southern Italian villages, archetypical peasant societies, is matriarchal, and that the social structure of most other poor, relatively isolated Western communities in countries where the Catholic Church either dominates or is an outright state religion, is matriarchal. It is a *de facto* system, one that is felt by everyone, that functions every day, but is not codified and does not have to be recognized. It is simply there. There are no large decisions to be made by the men and day-by-day existence is left to the women, who unconsciously take over all the practical aspects of life. There are no others. Once a woman has power, however slight her influence appears to be outside the family, she consolidates it into a hold over her sons stronger than that famous boast of the Jesuits. Only death will loosen it, but already her daughter-in-law has learned the art of day-by-day living and day-by-day power and has tied her sons to her as firmly as though they were still swaddled. She has also slowly replaced her husband's mother, and he, accustomed as he is to the strength of women, does not notice it. He would, in fact, insist with aggressive pride, "*In casa mia, comando io!*" In my house, *I* command.

It is my opinion and I offer it now for several reasons.

1) As I have already said, I fear the seemingly inevitable manipulation of social myths. More and more we are trusting social scientists to plan our "social priorities," design programs and even direct them. At best social problems are difficult to understand, much less solve: at least our premises must be just. In my experience patriarchal dominance has never been absolute, is often nonexistent. I think the rigid dogma needs qualification.

2) Now that we have efficiently arranged for the *disgregazione della società* of Southern Italy and the elimination of the peasant as such, he will be more than ever an intriguing subject of study. I can imagine investigations into his adaptation to industrial society, into his residual vestiges of peasant mentality, as though it were the sacroiliac or the appendix, into his new buying habits, his new sex habits, his new ambitions for his children, and so on. They will be followed by treatises recommending aids for the habilitation of the peasant into the myriad aspects of industrial society — all based on a constant which is out of focus and therefore doomed to repeat its own aberration in new, distorted myths.

3) If social scientists are to have so much to say about how society functions and how it should be improved, they may have to use more common sense and understanding, less creative methodology, and rediscover man. He is, if I have not misunderstood, the subject of their work. They say nothing about him if they knit his traits together, like stitches, casting them off and on, dropping and slipping them to fit a new, fashionable pattern, no matter how esthetically satisfying to the designer. I realize that the lives of social scientists are sometimes ordered by that old academic law of "publish or perish,"

but even that does not excuse the mangling of historical fact to fit prefabricated conclusions. As, for instance, the very same authors who wielded "A Principal Components Factor Analysis with Verimax Rotation," ignoring, surely not ignorant of the last hundred years of Italian history, can pontificate:

> The economy of the Mexican peasant village is similar to that of villages in Southern Italy. The two societies share many psychological characteristics. The main difference lies in the fact of the minor role of alcoholism in Southern Italy and in the fact that men rarely leave their families. It is our hypothesis that the reason for this difference is that Italy has had centuries of unbroken patriarchal dominance, while the Mexican patriarchy has been undermined.[*]

Via! The lonely (and inconvenient) years of millions of Southern Italian husbands and grandfathers are eradicated. They never left their wives and children, they never went to Australia, South America and Canada. They never went to New York, Newark, Philadelphia, Boston, Chicago or San Francisco, to the New World where the streets were paved with gold, at least on the other side of town. They did not struggle for ten years, twenty years alone, before they could either bring their families to join them or returned home in defeat. Did the authors never encounter the vast printed documentation of how such men came to the New World, how they lived, of the structures of the "Little Italys" that were their ghettos? Or did they ignore it to preserve the dogma that says Western peasant culture is patriarchal? Perhaps

[*] *Social Character in a Mexican Village*, Erich Fromm and Michael Maccoby, Prentice-Hall, Englewood Cliffs, N.J. 1970. Page 171.

once they had dared to suggest that the Mexican male is not quite dominant, they ran out of courage. And what did undermine that patriarchy? The absence of the men and the women's discovery that they could manage their decisions? Is there a positive, rather than a negative phrase for undermined patriarchy? Perhaps limited matriarchy? Or has cant replaced reason?

I have been a bystander while Southern Italy has telescoped one hundred and fifty years into the last twenty. At times only a long dim tunnel seemed to connect it to this century. Now light is showing, probably neon, but light. Soon Southern Italy will trundle out of the dark into the murky world of today. Perhaps it can match depression with recession and for the saddest of all reasons achieve something approximating equality with the rest of Italy. What I have watched is the slow extinction of one of the last feudal societies. I do not have to imagine a past; I lived it. The present is documented every day in the newspapers, and the future is no longer just a shadow, but has a shape, however amorphous. During those twenty years I talked to the women of the South and listened to them and watched them.

In any formal situation the women will go to great lengths not to mar the picture a husband has given of himself and his supremacy within the family. "What he said is right," or "Don't ask me, ask him," are the only answers they give and then sit, their faces blank as potatoes, their hands crossed in their laps. I was present when a woman, a widow I know extremely well, answered an interviewer with all solemnity: No, I would never do anything my mother did not approve of. Her face was smooth and relaxed, her eyes, except that she would not look at me, seemed entirely without guile, and yet I knew that twenty-five years before she had taken over the management of the family. She was twenty then. Her mother was ill and would never again be strong, and there were six children younger than she to settle in the world. Even today they come to her for help. She found work for her brothers, negotiated their agreements for them, licked them when they balked and loaned them money when they needed it — without ever asking her mother's approval. In fact the mother has seldom tried to act; when she does her sons listen. Twice in the last fifteen years she has called the family together for an announcement. Both times she wished to disown her daughter because she had decided to do something of which the mother did not approve. Both times the daughter has, regretfully, proceeded with her plans, and had the rather bitter pleasure of watching her brothers, who had sided with their mother, come back one by one, not to apologize openly, but to ask advice or borrow money. Incidentally, she is not a great favorite of their wives. When I asked her why she had answered the interviewer as she did, she smiled. "The Commandments say Honor thy father and thy mother, don't they? No reason to let anyone know what happens inside the family. It's bad enough that it happens." She feels, as I suspect a great many others do, that she must qualify as a supporter of "what is right" in front of outsiders. Public conventions, even those of the Christian ethic, protect her, are in a sense camouflage, without requiring her literal loyalty. Admittedly it is difficult for a man or a team of men and women in a village only briefly to have more than the most fleeting contact with such women. I do not know that many have tried.

The people of the mountains are dour men and women whose faces erode early into deep furrows and whose bodies are old before their time. It is said they are fierce, unfriendly, but I have not found them so. They are not the vivacious Italians of tourist brochures. They wait, offering nothing of themselves, to find out who you are and what reason you can offer for your intrusion into their lonely eyrie. No one comes from the outside world by choice: doctors, teachers, midwives, even government clerks in their midst consider themselves in exile. Peasants repay this arrogance with silence. Until they are given reason to act otherwise, they are always courteous. Tradition requires that they offer what hospitality they can afford and they do with great dignity, but their confidence comes slowly. Too often, they have learned, it is a mistake to trust.

3

One evening recently I sat again by the stove in Chichella's little front room. After a raw cold day, the wind had come up, but was, for once, a faint-hearted intruder, content to jiggle the doors, and blow lugubrious, moaning chords through the jambs. Below in the courtyard tin cans shunted about, clonking into walls, tinkling and jangling over the stones. Surrounded by those lonely, random sounds, which are to me the foghorns of the dark, I puzzled over the South, not for the first time, nor for the last.

Next door in the kitchen Chichella was making a third and final attempt to "iron dry" her son's work trousers. After so many years she is accustomed to my silences. They are no longer the first mysterious symptoms of melancholia, but a minor vice she must humor. She tells people I need time to rearrange my ideas. From her tone it is obviously a futile operation, almost an affliction, like that of the compulsive furniture mover or the gentle demented creature who is happy sorting and resorting the same pile of miscellaneous junk. The truth is that she tolerates my silences only as long as she does not feel excluded, a state she sees no reason to endure for anyone. Chichella has never been passive, and I knew that in a few minutes she would stick her head around the corner and say, "*Eh beh . . . ?*" which is her verbal shorthand for "Well, what is it this time?" And I would have to admit that it was the same puzzle of other years: the South — how to reconcile the split image of appearance and reality.

People tell me that everything in the South has changed. What they mean is that everything looks different. They want to believe that is enough. If it is, why, then, is the Southerner's average annual income ($700) still half that of the Northerner? And why is the Southerner's only choice still genteel starvation at home or emigration? New buildings, schools, "Self-Service" (the entire phrase carefully left in English) grocery stores, policemen in comic-opera uniforms who scowl at passing cars, and new streetlights that buzz all night, what have they . . .

"*Eh beh . . . ?*" came Chichella's exasperated voice at my shoulder. I had to admit that I was worrying the same problem, like an old, cynical cat who suspects the catnip mouse she has been offered is only a decoy to distract her. "So?" She tried not to sound impatient. "Is that part of what you're doing?"

I told her, as I have always told her, the truth,

knowing that her perception would compensate for any theory she might lack. I explained my conviction that whatever quality of life there has been in the South, whatever security, has depended on the women. Chichella listens as though all life around her has ceased and only your ideas are, for the moment, real. Those black peppercorn eyes seem to search your brain for ravelings. More than once I have heard my voice dwindle away to stammers, because I have tripped over my own fallacy, and I have looked up 'to find Chichella smiling, relieved that I have found my own omission. I have never known, I only suspect that she had already recognized it. I do know, however, that other times, when I have been mesmerized by my own theories, she has waited for me to finish and then said, "Of course, I am no professor, but . . ." Each reason will be a demolition ball and slowly my structure will crumble.

That night, as I talked, she pulled up a low, rush-bottomed chair that she likes, spread her legs well apart, put her elbows on her knees and then leaned over to press her hands up against the stove. To get as close to heat as possible is a lifelong habit; her eyes never left my face. When I had finished, she just sat, still looking at me, still moving her hands about on the hot stove, and I thought she had not understood. I mentioned people we both know, as examples, but she interrupted me.

"I understand. Don't worry, I understand. I want to think about it for a minute, that's all. You see, for *you* it's something to watch and study, but it's my *life*. You see it one way, and maybe I don't see it at all, or maybe —" She stopped and leaned forward until her chin rested on her hands on top of the stove. Finally she looked up at me, and beyond, as though searching for words, which then came out in a rush, Chichella's organized, succinct kind of rush.

"I don't know how to say it exactly, but do you remember when you first came, they ('They' are always the government) were giving peasants money for patching up their houses — the *outsides* of their houses? Well, didn't they look pretty with all that new plaster and paint? Do *you* think the people inside lived any different because there was plaster and paint on the outside? I can tell you they didn't. That's how change has been here. They don't want the *miseria* to show, so we're all paint and plaster and new buildings and new roads and cars and fancy clothes. Sure! All of that. Water comes out of pipes, when it comes, and two buses go to Potenza every day, but the fight is still the same — to eat, to stay alive."

She hesitated long enough for me to think she had finished, but I should have known better. She never leaves loose ends.

"As for the women. Put any label you want on it. It amounts to the same thing: we do whatever no one else has done. That's what we're taught; that's what we're supposed to do. Men work and talk about politics. We do the rest. If we have to decide, that's fair too. Why should we do all the work and not decide? We decide, but we don't have to talk about it in the Piazza. Call that power, if you want to. To us it's just killing work. That's what our lives are. We're born knowing it. And these young girls — my girls, all the girls — they're spoiled. No, they're ruined. 'I want this,' 'I want that,' 'I have a right to this,' is all they know. They won't work. It's beneath them. The schools taught them that. Taught them their rights. Only there's no easy way to get them, so they're going to wait for the miracle. They may starve, waiting

227

like *signore*. They don't know yet that this isn't a world of miracles. It's a world of work. It's that simple. If you want something, you work and sometimes even then . . . They don't know yet that miracles only happen in church."

And so the last word belongs to Chichella, which is as it should be.

A Life Cycle

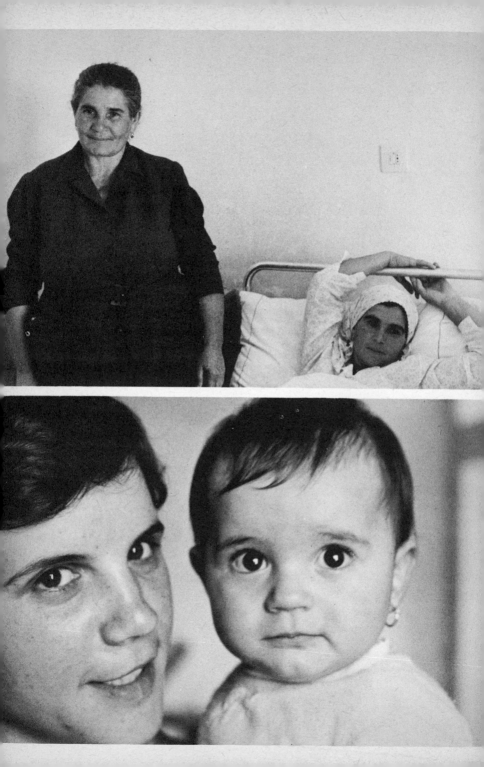

ANN CORNELISEN was born in Cleveland, Ohio, and educated at Vassar College. In 1954 she went to Florence intending to study archaeology; instead, she spent ten years with the Save the Children Fund, setting up nurseries in impoverished villages of southern Italy. She is the author of two other books on the south of Italy, *Torregreca* and *Vendetta of Silence*, a novel. In 1974 she received a special award from the National Institute of Arts and Letters. At present she lives in a thirteenth-century house in Cortona, Italy.